Choose Your
DESTINY

To my new friend

David

from Past. Anyifo

Choose Your
DESTINY

how your decisions affect your life

ANGELO SCANNAPIECO

Originally published in Italy with the title:
Scegli il tuo destino
by Destiny Image™ Europe
Via della Scafa 29/14
Città S.Angelo (Pe) - Italy
© Copyright 2010—Angelo Scannapieco

"Changing the World, One Book at a Time."

This book and all other Evangelista Media™ and Destiny Image™ Europe books are available at Christian bookstores and distributors worldwide.

To order products, or for any other correspondence:

EVANGELISTA MEDIA™ srl
Via della Scafa, 29/14
65013 Città Sant'Angelo (Pe) – Italy
Tel. +39 085 4716623 • Fax: +39 085 9090113
Email: info@evangelistamedia.com
Or reach us on the Internet: www.evangelistamedia.com

ISBN 13: 978-88-97896-13-5
ISBN 13 Ebook: 978-88-97896-14-2

For Worldwide Distribution, Printed in the U.S.A.
1 2 3 4 5 6 / 15 14 13 12

ACKNOWLEDGMENTS

First of all, my deepest gratitude goes to our Lord Jesus Christ because when I met Him, He changed my life for the better for eternity.

Then, my sincere appreciation goes to:

My wife, Chiara. You are my precious support, always full of great care for me and our children: Selene, Tabita, and Gabriele.

My parents. Thank you for understanding how important it was for me to follow the way that the Lord had put in my heart, giving me full freedom to do so.

All the members of the Gesù Vive church. You are much more than a church and a vision: you are a very precious united group of people.

Federica. Thank you for your patient and outstanding collaboration in the typing of this book.

Last, I want to thank all the men of God who, throughout the years, have sown eternal values within my heart.

CONTENTS

INTRODUCTION

THE MESSAGE OF LIFE

It is with my great joy that this book is in your hands. It is the fruit of a lifetime dedicated to studying, meditating, and putting into practice the Word of God.

Over the years, I have preached a series of messages to my congregation aimed at confirming the profound truth that putting biblical principles into practice every day brings about real changes in life. Such firm belief drove me to revise and write out those messages so as to create this book, fruit of a wealth of experience useful to understand the true nature of God's love for the edification of those who long for fullness of life.

The messages chosen analyze the period in which David and his men were obliged to take refuge in the cave of Adullam because of King Saul's ruthless persecution. Like those men, I have often felt powerless too; but in the wake of many biblical warriors belonging to the army of God, I have chosen to see myself through *God's eyes*. This has enabled me to succeed in every deed and to overcome the most critical situations. Thanks to the revelation of what God has done for me, what He is doing, and especially what He will continue to do in the future, I have refused to consider myself defeated.

God wants to do for you today what He did for David in the past. He still keeps His promises toward those who believe in His Son's deeds and who rely upon Him in every circumstance by faith in His Word, acting according to what it says.

If you are moved by such desire, this book will be helpful. God finds great joy in pouring out His blessings and grace over His children.

What you are about to read by no means reflects the speeches of a "religious" person, but rather my continuous desire to put biblical teachings into practice in my daily life. Therefore, the following pages describe an actual lifestyle that enables us to be more than conquerors. We will carefully observe clear, strong, and solid examples with which we can identify and in which we are to believe with all our hearts. This is the only way we can follow in these men's footsteps, or better in the footsteps left us by God so that we can learn how to abound and prosper in every area of our lives.

It is with this spirit of courage and boldness, typical of those who allowed Christ to abide in them, that I took on this literary adventure addressed to all.

This book is the sincere expression of a simple man who has chosen to live by faith. Biblical principles are always valid for *whoever* believes. Therefore, it is addressed to *whoever* wants to live by faith in a tangible way.

The Gospel is a message of life to be spread everywhere and with any means. For this reason, my family, my church, and I do our utmost to make the Truth known through messages, Bible school, television programs, Internet, theatrical performances, and the European Conference of Faith *(Convegno Europeo della Fede)* in which both foreign and Italian speakers participate.

I am sure that this book will be of encouragement for you, for all those who want to overcome adverse circumstances in an apparently meaningless life, and those who want to see their dreams come true and their aims accomplished. I chose to write in a colloquial style because, in these twenty years of ministry, I have noticed how the evangelical message is most effective when the seed of the Word is sown in an environment where the hearts of both the announcer and the listener meet.

By my heart meeting yours in direct communication, this book will produce real and lasting changes in your life.

Pastor Angelo Scannapieco

David's family and all those who were in distress
gathered around him in the cave and he chose his destiny—
he chose to become their captain.

[They] *went down to the rock to David,*
into the cave of Adullam...
(1 Chronicles 11:15).

...And that Rock was Christ (1 Corinthians 10:4).

Chapter One

FOLLOW THE WAY,
FIND THE LIGHT

Train and Equip Yourself—
You Will Reach the Peak

Then Jesus spoke to them again, saying, "I am the light of the world. He who follows Me shall not walk in darkness, but have the light of life" (John 8:12).

Who, or rather what decides your destiny? Perhaps fate or fatalism?

Consider this. How can a kitten possibly die of hunger if there is a plate full of food in front of it? Some would say it is *destiny's fault*.

Not necessarily! All it would take to save the kitten would be a simple action: to break the food into bits.

Would a newborn lamb be able to survive separated from the rest of the flock and its nursing mother? Some would say with no hesitation that *its destiny is sure death*.

Not necessarily! In fact, all it would take would be a baby bottle and some milk.

My wife and I experienced both these situations while our powerless children stood by observing their parents change possible outcomes through prompt actions.

Since the day I accepted Jesus as my Lord, the viewpoint according to which there is a preordained universal natural order to which everything is subject and from which nothing and nobody can escape, is no longer compatible with mine. Now that I know God through a personal relationship, I know that He has destined me to reign in my present and future life, giving me both the ability and the possibility to exert dominion over any adverse circumstance, changing what might seem an inevitable destiny. The latter is commonly thought of as *fate*, that is a *fixed sequence* of inevitable and invariable *events*. However, the course of events can and must be changed in function of *spiritual laws* by which we are to let ourselves be led in order to grow in our faith and in our closeness to God.

Psalm 107 verse 30 says that God brings us safely to the desired haven. This image highlights how God does not ignore our desires. Actually, as a loving Father, He keeps them in mind guiding us through places of peace and rest and leading us to the final aim—our award!

Several years ago, I went hiking with some friends on the Gran Paradiso to observe chamoises and steinbocks in their natural environment. While going up the mountain, we saw a herd; and in order to follow it, we left the path, separating from each other. Our adventure suddenly turned into a tragedy. The memory of those moments is still alive in me today. I found myself in front of a peak that I had to climb with great effort with the sole help of my arms. The difficulty was enormous owing to my tiredness. I started shouting in the attempt to call my friends' attention, but it was useless because we were all busy trying to get out of that situation unhurt.

I decided to retrace my steps. I kept thinking, *I'll go down the slope being careful where I put my feet and somehow I'll reach the valley. The valley is at the bottom of the slope; little by little, I'll make it.* However, I soon had to change my mind. I experienced how risky it is to go down a slope not following a path.

I found myself going about here and there looking for a path, a gleam of light in order to come out of the thick vegetation. The brambles scratched my whole body. The more I moved toward the valley, the thicker the vegetation became, preventing me from seeing. It so happened that all of a sudden I was on the edge of a precipice.

I was exhausted. Once again I changed direction, always going toward the valley. I finally heard the sound of a river. I started walking in that direction until I reached it. When I saw it, I said to myself, *The river goes down toward valley!* I entered the water with my clothes on and followed the stream until I started to recognize some familiar points. My nightmare was finally over. But what was my state of mind by the end of that terrible experience? My joy, my strength, and my expectations had vanished, while exhaustion and disappointment had taken over and had led my steps.

How can we help someone who is in a similar situation? Someone who may not be lost in a forest, but may be lost in life's everyday brambles and thick vegetation where it is hard for him or her to see ahead. We need to:

- *Strengthen the weak*

- *Take care of the sick*

- *Medicate the injured*

- *Lead the lost back home*

- *Seek the lost*

This is how God encourages us to act.

To strengthen those who are weak means to make them strong and firm. Everything starts with an action, so give the weak something to eat! At a spiritual level this means to feed them with the Word of God.

To take care of the sick means to look after their person providing them with a continuous treatment through the Word of God, the medicine that cures everything and everyone.

To medicate the injured means to soothe their injuries with attention and tenderness and to wrap them with love bandages.

To lead the lost back home is not simple. There are people who, owing to their many disappointments, have lost the capability to love and have become stern and harsh. Others have lost sight of their main aim in life and have ended up following temporary ones or those that someone else has considered right for them. Others yet have followed bad companies getting lost in blind alleys. What can we do to help those whose hearts, minds, or even entire lives are lost? Jesus is the way for all of these to find what they have lost.

To seek the lost can mean finding a person who has gotten lost in the twists and turns of life, or finding what this person has lost along the way. Whatever the case, what everybody really needs is light, because only by making light in the darkness we can find what has been lost.

Through this book, chapter after chapter, my desire is to guide you in a wonderful journey. May you find new strength, climb to the peak of your life, conquer it, and raise the flag of victory!

Chapter Two

TAKE THE FIRST STEP

A Man Ready to Do God's Will

David therefore departed from there and escaped to the cave of Adullam. So when his brothers and all his father's house heard it, they went down there to him. And everyone who was in distress, everyone who was in debt, and everyone who was discontented gathered to him. So he became captain over them. And there were about four hundred men with him (1 Samuel 22:1-2).

In this chapter we will look at David's situation focusing on his strength, which is what drove me to write this book.

My desire is to present David as a common man with the same difficulties we all face in life. Page after page, we will discover how he was able to overcome every obstacle to the point of becoming the leader of an entire people. A careful analysis of First Samuel 22:1-2 shows us how 400 people gathered around David and how they were all in great distress. If you have ever had a direct experience with someone in distress, you certainly know the kind and amount of difficulties one faces to help such a person recover. Multiply a single experience of that kind by 400, and you will have a clear picture of David's situation.

The Scriptures say that David was a *man after God's heart*[1] willing to listen, careful in keeping his eyes set on God and, especially, willing to obey, fully believing that God's will was the best thing for him and for those men who had gathered around him.

They all had something in common: they were discontented, in distress, and in debt. A difficult situation in front of which David chose to react in a way pleasing to God, making him deserve the biblical classification of a *man after God's heart*. He did not go off and leave those men, who were losers according to human categories, but rather preferred to consider their hearts as raw material on which he could work.

In fact, David knew that it is impossible to come out of difficulties in an instant, and that the key to success in every situation is to have a heart ready to follow God's will.

Men in Distress

Problems do not disappear magically in an instant. Not only David was in a precarious situation, but he also had many individuals gathering around him in a state similar to his. Although we do not know what kind of difficulties these 400 people were facing, we can imagine that they did not consider themselves men and women of God endowed with the supernatural ability to face the challenges of life.[2] They probably kept repeating to themselves that they had no hope.

Perhaps you are in a similar situation, and you feel unable and are afraid of not making it. But the Bible is full of examples of how God shows His favor toward those who let Him lead them. You need God's wisdom to exercise inner knowledge and overcome every day's obstacles.[3]

Perhaps you think that you can make it in your own strength or thanks to the knowledge you have acquired through your education, which however often reveals to be insufficient even if good in itself. Therefore, the wisest thing to do is to use another kind of wisdom— God's wisdom. One of the gifts He gives largely is the Word of wisdom, so ask Him for it.[4] I can guarantee that one word of His is sufficient to throw light on your problems, and what you have not obtained fighting in your own strength, you will obtain through divine wisdom.

Who knows how many of us are overwhelmed by difficulties and have decided in their hearts to go down to the cave of Adullam, just like those 400 men who said to themselves, *In that place there is a man after God's heart; if we stay close to him, we will be able to learn from him!* They considered David a man who followed God's ways, and who therefore could help them.[5]

Men in Debt

Men seriously in debt took refuge in the cave.

Several years ago, a young couple with small children started attending our church. The wife was a fervent believer, while her husband still showed some reservation in surrendering to the Lord. The two formed a nice couple and an apparently serene family. One day the woman found the courage to talk to us openly, confessing that things were not exactly as they seemed because her husband was addicted to video poker games. The vice had led him to dedicate more time to playing than working; so their income had decreased, and the couple was buried in debts. As if it were not enough, even the man's attentions toward his family had diminished. He was no longer able to stay away from the games, slave of a vicious circle: the more money he lost, the more he played to make up for it.

In time, we managed to grow close to that man, who opened his heart to us and especially managed to open his heart to God, putting that desperate situation in His powerful and merciful hands.

Today I am happy to testify that he is blessed both in his family life and in his working life, and is a great example for his children and for the church.

From this experience we can see how this man started out trusting me, and then, having put his trust in my person, he came to trust God. The same thing happened between David and the 400 men. They decided to trust and to follow David, and ended up trusting God. How did this happen? What did David do to lead these men into the Lord's presence?

He never said, "Come to me and I'll pay your debts!" just like you will never hear your pastor say, "Come to me, and I'll pay everything you owe!"

Only today's *Sauls*, those who take on the name of the fateful king who symbolizes those who do not walk according to the Spirit, can say similar things. Those who follow God's will do not pay your debts, but teach you how to present yourself to God, the only One who has the necessary money to pay them.[6] When you find men or women who want to teach you how to present your difficult financial situation and your problems to God, gather around them and follow them with the certainty that God's bank will never fail.

Men like Saul make his same mistake. When Saul found out that those men were gathering around David, he tried to divert them in every way possible.

Here is what the Bible says in First Samuel 22:7:

> *Then Saul said to his servants who stood about him, "Hear now, you Benjamites! Will the son of Jesse* [David] *give every one of you fields and vineyards, and make you all captains of thousands and captains of hundreds?"*

Sauls act according to the schemes of this world, making great promises they are not able to keep. Saul basically was saying: "Will the son of Jesse ever be able to give you fields and vineyards? Come to me and I'll give them to you! Come to me and I'll make you captains of thousands and captains of hundreds."

This is the way Sauls reason today, but certainly not those who follow God. David made no such promise to those who wanted to follow him. He never said, "Come to me and I'll give you fields, vineyards, houses and I'll make you captains of thousands and captains of hundreds." In the same way, no pastor would state such foolishness. If you are thinking of asking your church to help you pay your debts, it will be difficult to receive this kind of support. Instead, your pastor will teach you how to go to God to receive help directly from His hands.[7]

A pastor's assignment is to teach people how to find help in God. In fact, He is always ready to give with generosity according to His character.

I invite you to reflect on this following truth: God gave us what He had that was most precious, His Son Jesus Christ! The Scriptures say, "How shall He not with Him also freely give us all things?" (Rom. 8:32). If God gave us Jesus, He is also ready to give us everything we need. A pastor's assignment, therefore, is to teach people how to go to God so that He can guide them and take care of the solution to their problems, even the financial ones. In every church there are members facing economic difficulties. They need to learn at the *School of Adullam*, following David's example, how to come out of their debts using the Word of God, asking for His help and having faith in Him. The cave of Adullam was an actual school of faith for those 400 men who entered full of distress and debts, but came out delivered and more than conquerors. This is what the Scriptures teach us.[8] However, they had to spend some time in the cave with David.

Men in Discontent

The men who entered the cave were also discontented. The fact of being discontented or dissatisfied entails a certain degree of sadness. In turn, sadness takes joy away from us. When we lose our joy, we are also deprived of another vital element for the attainment of our destiny—strength. The Bible defines strength in these terms: "The joy of the Lord is your strength."[9]

Think of the joy David must have felt when he saw the Ark of the Covenant brought back to Jerusalem. In Second Samuel 6:16 we read, "Michal, Saul's daughter, looked through a window and saw King David leaping and whirling before the Lord...."

David wanted the Ark back in Jerusalem and to honor God's presence, represented by the Ark.

Today God's presence is within *us*! It is wonderful to see an entire church leap and whirl before the Father, while His presence and anointing[10] deliver us from our burdens and we are pervaded by His joy that enables us to rise above our circumstances. It is exactly in those moments that people start coming out of their difficulties. The weak start seeing themselves with new eyes, and those who are under the burden of debts start seeing that there is Someone who can really help them.

Each one of the 400 men in the cave with David was in distress; but at the school of faith, they all learned how to come out of their problems. The same will happen to you while attending your church.

Your pastor cannot give you a house or the money you need. However, he can help you meet God and come out of your state of need through His Word.

CRY OUT TO THE LORD: PSALM 142

Let's have a look at Psalm 142 remembering where it was written. Its subtitle says, "A contemplation of David. A prayer when he was in the cave."

This psalm was written by David when he was in the cave of Adullam, after he had lost everything and everybody. He had defeated Goliath and received honors for this feat, but now he was in the cave of Adullam alone with his memories. He no longer had any personal and material support, let alone wealth. He had lost everything. All he had were God's promises.

Have you ever found yourself in a situation like David's?

By observing his behavior and actions, we can see how he overcame the situation and accomplished his destiny.

> *I cry out to the Lord with my voice; with my voice to the Lord I make my supplication. I pour out my complaint before Him; I declare before Him my trouble. When my spirit was overwhelmed within me, then You knew my path. In the way in which I walk they have secretly set a snare for me. Look on my right hand and see, for there is no one who acknowledges*

me; refuge has failed me; no one cares for my soul. I cried out to You, O Lord: I said, "You are my refuge, my portion in the land of the living. Attend to my cry, for I am brought very low; deliver me from my persecutors, for they are stronger than I. Bring my soul out of prison, that I may praise Your name; the righteous shall surround me, for You shall deal bountifully with me" (Psalm 142).

Let's read Psalm 142 more closely. Verse 1 says, "I cry out to the Lord with my voice; with my voice to the Lord I make my supplication." As soon as he took refuge in the cave, David cried out in extreme poverty. Whom did he cry out to? To the 400 men? No! He cried out to the Lord. He did not ask for help from his 400 men; he did not rely on them, but only on God.

"I cry out to the Lord with my voice; with my voice to 400 men I make my supplication." Are these the words he pronounced? No! Instead, he said: "…with my voice to the Lord I make my supplication [for His help]."

The cave is a place where you cry out to God. In the cave of Adullam you cry out to the Lord. You do not cry out to receive help from men, but from God. Therefore, this is the first lesson that those men learned.

Now for the second verse, "I pour out my complaint before these 400 men." Are these the words you read in the Bible? No! Is it before men that you are supposed to pour out your complaint? No! David actually said, "I pour out my complaint before *Him*."

It is as if he were saying, "I am in great distress, I am discontented, full of debts, but I pour out my complaint before God." And he continues: "I declare before *Him* my trouble." Before whom? Before the 400 men? No, before *Him*, "I declare before God my trouble."

Learn from David; do what he did. We should all follow his example. We are to follow the example of the lives of the great men whom the Bible talks about, who accomplished their destinies. David was a man of success, an overcomer. Without any doubt he made mistakes, but we need to imitate "the way" he triumphed, and avoiding repeating his same mistakes.

If you really want to learn how to come out of distress, discontent, and debts, you need to observe David and his men. They went into God's presence, cried out to Him and poured out their complaint before Him!

Defeat the Enemy from Behind

Let's continue reading Psalm 142. Verse 3 says, "When my spirit was overwhelmed within me, then You knew my path. In the way in which I walk they [the enemies] have secretly set a snare for me." The Psalm invites us to be careful because there are snares along our way. Just think of when the Hebrews escaped from Egypt. The Bible mentions how the enemy followed the Israelites when they started to walk on dry land owing to the miraculous departing of the waters while they walked through. The enemy never stops along the shore watching us go by, but follows us trying to hinder our way toward freedom, while we take our first steps through the sea of problems.

God is still able today to open up the sea of problems in front of our eyes so that we can come out delivered. He will open up the sea of problems in front of your eyes, but your enemies will continue to pursue you. You have to learn how to let the sea close back up behind you so that the enemy may be submerged. The same power that opened it will be at work to close it.

The school of faith of the cave of Adullam is the local church where we learn how to accomplish God's promises by faith. This is where we make His promises ours, reminding Him about them every day in prayer together with other brothers and sisters. David and his men learned how to walk by faith together.

They learned how to present their difficulties to God, instead of complaining among each other.

It is always easy to complain. I tell you my problems and you tell me yours, with the only result that our lives will always be more problematic. Instead, we should surround ourselves with brothers and sisters who encourage us by saying, "I made it thanks to the Lord's help who showed me, step by step, what to do. Simply believe, and you will make it as well!"

Yes, you will make it! All you have to do is listen to the words of encouragement and guidance of those who have overcome situations similar to yours. Then your faith will grow, and you will make God's promises yours![11]

What to Do When There Is No Escape

In Psalm 142:4 we read, "Look to the right and see; for there is no one who regards me; there is no escape for me; no one cares for my soul" (New American Standard Bible).

This verse is saying, "I am in distress, I am discontented, I am full of debts." The psalmist here recognizes that there is no escape.

These were the same feelings the Hebrews felt during their escape from Egypt, when they found themselves in front of the Red Sea. They had the Egyptians behind and the sea in front. They could not advance; but at the same time, they could not go back either. There was no escape. What do you do in such a case?

Let's continue with verse 5: "I cried out to You, O Lord: I said, 'You are my refuge, my portion in the land of the living.'" Repeat these words out loud: "I cry out to You, O Lord!" The church needs to learn how to cry out to God and not to man, because man's help is good for little or nothing. When you learn how to cry out to God, you receive real help wherever you are. David cried out to the Lord using his tongue as a rudder to make the ship of his life change direction, moving it from misery toward God. He said, "I am in great distress, I am discontented, I am full of debts, but You, Lord, are my refuge, You are my portion in the land of the living."

You might assert that you already have everything in God, that you know that you are going to heaven where you will spend eternity, and that when you get there you will lack in nothing. But this is not what David said. He declared: "You are my portion in the land of the living!"

It is true that there is a rich future inheritance attending each one of us, but David needed something from which he could draw in that difficult moment when he was wretched and lacking in everything. He had 400 people with him, but he learned how to cry out to God to receive everything he needed. The cave became his school of faith. He was responsible for those men, just as you are for your family. All he could do and had to do was cry out to the Lord. By imitating David, those in the cave learned how to cry out to God.

Verse 6 says, "Listen to my cry, for I am in desperate need; rescue me from those who pursue me, for they are too strong for me" (NIV). With these words David recognized that he was in desperate need, but he reminded himself and God, "You are my refuge."

"I am in desperate need, but You are my refuge. Rescue me from those who pursue me, for they are too strong for me. I take refuge in You, because I know that You are a safe refuge for me." These are the right words that you should cry out to God when you are in desperate need.

There Is Prosperity in God's Promises

Let's read verse 7, "Bring my soul out of prison, that I may praise Your name; the righteous shall surround me, for You shall deal bountifully with me." David was in a cave, he had nothing, he was discontented, full of problems, together with 400 people all in his same situation. So David said this prayer, which was not based on his misery, but on his trust in God's power and provision. Through this prayer, he raised himself from the state of misery up to God, and cried out to the Lord saying, "For you shall deal bountifully with me."

Repeat these same words, "God shall deal bountifully with me."

The Bible says, "*Surely* goodness and mercy shall follow *me* [shall follow my person] all the days of my life" (Ps. 23:6).

David was a man after God's heart who had learned how to *cry out* to the Lord when everything was going wrong. "You shall deal bountifully with me." He still did not possess the wealth he talked about, but he could declare it because he had taken the first step directing his faith and his tongue toward God's promises.

The 400 men with him were still in distress, in debt, and discontented, but by following David they took the first step as well; they entered the school of faith to learn how to cry out to God, trusting that He knew how to take care of them.

Therefore, they started to find the way out of their problems, while their complaints gave way to the joy of the Lord. They did not start rejoicing after their problems were solved, but rather while they were still totally buried in them. In the midst of fire, they set their eyes upon the Lord, their Deliverer, and the Holy One of Israel.

You need to set your eyes on God's promises as well, more than ever.

Let's have a look at Second Corinthians 5:21, "For He [God] made Him [Jesus] who knew no sin to be sin *for us*, that *we* might become the righteousness of God in Him."

Jesus was made sin for *all* of us and for *each one* of us. Therefore, there is a promise of salvation and redemption waiting for us. Jesus paid the price of your redemption; therefore, you can make those promises yours. If you are without hope, there is good news for you—you can come out of your desperation! However, in order to do so, you have to enter the cave of Adullam, the school of faith, and become a member of a local church that believes in the Word of God and preaches the truth. God is faithful and keeps all of His promises![12]

In Galatians 3:13-14 the Bible says:

> *Christ has redeemed us from the curse of the law, having become a curse for us...that the blessing of Abraham might come upon the Gentiles in Christ Jesus....*

Jesus Christ became a curse *for us* but especially for *each one* of us. On the cross, Jesus took the curse upon Himself so that *you* could inherit the blessing.

You were blessed when Jesus became a curse. Why then do you still live in fear? Why are you afraid of your future? Why are you afraid that something bad can happen to you? Why are you afraid of the darkness and of the shadows surrounding you?

Jesus took the curse upon the cross. *He has already paid.* There is nothing left for you to pay. You are free from *every* curse, from *every* fear, from *every* concern. You have to start searching the Lord by using your mouth and tongue, and remembering His promises in His presence. This will give you strength and will keep you in a fighting attitude. It will get you into the school of faith and out of your problems!

Besides, the Bible says in First Peter 2:24, "Who Himself bore our sins in His own body on the tree, that *we*, having died to sins, might live for righteousness by whose stripes you were healed."

Jesus bore our diseases so that we might receive *healing.* Jesus bore our diseases so that we might have faith and be healed. Jesus Himself bore *your* diseases so that you could claim healing and the solutions to your problems.

The Value of a Single Cry

Let's read Second Corinthians 8:9: "For you know the grace of our Lord Jesus Christ, that though He was rich, yet for your sakes He became poor, that you through His poverty might become rich." The term *rich* here indicates the fact that God puts His provision at our disposal to meet all of our needs. Richness and prosperity are not limited to our finances. In fact, we could be rich but our marriages could be in crises, making us the poorest among the poor.

Money cannot buy happiness. True joy comes from feeling totally loved and wanted by God.

Those 400 people in distress learned how to cry out to the Lord, relying on His promises, and God delivered them from their misery. Those who were buried in debts turned to God. They did not have a church or a pastor to go to; they cried out to God and said, "Lord, it is written that You became *poor* so that we could be rich *in You.* Now we cry out to You! All finances are Yours. You blessed the earth with all blessings so that we could be blessed! Thank You, Lord! Thank You because the windows of heaven are open."[13]

Trust in the Lord, not in yourself or in someone else. The Bible says, "Cursed is the man who trusts in man and makes flesh his strength, whose heart departs from the Lord" (Jeremiah 17:5), but it also says, "Blessed is the man who trusts in the Lord, and whose hope is the Lord" (Jeremiah 17:7).

My personal resources as well as my church's are limited, but they become unlimited when I rely on the infinite resources in heaven. Your resources will become unlimited only when you start trusting in God's infinite resources!

How to Become a Mighty Warrior

Let's go back to Psalm 142, verse 7, "Bring my soul out of prison, that I may praise Your name; the righteous shall surround me, for You shall deal bountifully with me." While they were still buried in distress, David started to declare the Word of God.

Were they already out of the cave? If they were, what was their situation? Did they still have unresolved problems? Were they desperate and in debt? If you go to church without ever finding the way out of your problems, you have found a form of religion but certainly not Jesus.

In fact, *He is the Good News*[14] of God, so that we may find and obtain salvation for every area of our lives: spirit, soul, and body!

Turning to God not only transforms our situations, but especially us, "These *were* the *chiefs* of David's *mighty warriors*—they, together with all Israel, gave his kingship *strong support* to extend it over the whole land, as the Lord had promised" (1 Chronicles 11:10 NIV).

What school transformed them into mighty warriors? The cave of Adullam.

Men and women discontented and full of problems were transformed at the school of faith becoming chiefs and mighty warriors.

David did not promise them one single thing; nonetheless, they received everything from the Lord. They became totally different from the people they used to be, being a great support for David.

Every pastor needs the valid support of mighty men and women in order to reach the place God has in mind for us. In fact, we cannot make it alone. Only together can we take possession of what God has prepared for us.

Do you believe that God will make you a mighty man or a mighty woman? Perhaps you still cannot see yourself in this light, but it is the way God sees you. The reason of this divergence of vision is because God does not see what your natural eyes see, rather, He looks at your heart;[15] He sees great value in you.

In First Chronicles 11:11 we read, "And this is the number of the mighty men whom David had." The Scriptures give us the list of those mighty warriors, among whom there was a chief of 30 captains who went out to fight against 300 men, overcoming them all: "He had lifted up his spear against three hundred, killed by him at one time."

God is great! You can overcome 300 enemies set out along your way! And this is just the beginning. However, you always need to remember that all of the honor goes to God because He is the One who gives the ability to accomplish such deeds.

Go to the Rock

In First Chronicles 11:15 we read, "Now three of the thirty chief men went down to the rock to David, into the cave of Adullam." These men went to David, to the rock in the cave of Adullam. Who was David's *rock*? Who is the rock in the New Testament? What does First Corinthians say about this rock?[16]

Jesus Christ is the Rock!

If you go to church and study the Word of God, you will learn how to go to the Rock, Christ, and rely on Him. It is not a matter of following a movement, a church, or supporting certain opinions. Going to the Rock equals turning to Christ! You will be able to come out of the cave like these men did, delivered from the problems you had before going in.

In First Chronicles 11:20 we read, "Abishai the brother of Joab was chief of another three. He had lifted up his spear against three hundred men, killed them, and won a name among these three." Here is another man who killed 300 enemies!

Now let's read verse 22, "Benaiah was the son of Jehoiada, the son of a valiant man from Kabzeel, who had done many deeds. He had killed two lion-like heroes of Moab. He also had gone down and killed a lion in the midst of a pit on a snowy day." Here is another man, son of a valiant man, author of great deeds.

The 400 men entered the cave as losers, but came out saying, "We will accomplish great deeds!" These men were able to change their destinies! The Word reminds us how Benaiah killed two men from Moab *who were like lions*, and how he *killed a lion in the midst of a pit on a snowy day.*

The enemy comes against you like a roaring lion,[17] but you can triumph owing to the victory you have in Jesus Christ! If you come out of the school of Adullam with this kind of faith, you will be strong and courageous. You entered the cave full of difficulties, but you will come out strong and victorious, delivered from the problems and debts you had before going in.

You will still have to face obstacles and problems along the way, but you will know how to overcome them!

An Example to Follow

The Lord led David and the 400 men out of the cave of defeat turning them into mighty warriors. The Bible talks about another group of people who decided to follow these mighty men's example and go to David.

People will see God's presence in you. You will be an example of what God can do in a person's life. Those around you will want to have what you have. Just like these men were a great light for their people, you can be a lighthouse for your nation.

"For at that time they came to David day by day to help him, until it was a great army, like the army of God" (1 Chronicles 12:22). When the world sees a glorious army of warriors come out of the school of faith, a church, or a Bible school, others will join the ranks to give praise, glory, and honor to God!

Chapter Three

ACT IN FAITH ON THE WORD

BE DELIVERED FROM YOUR ENEMIES: PSALM 57

Be merciful to me, O God, be merciful to me! For my soul trusts in You; and in the shadow of Your wings I will make my refuge, until these calamities have passed by. I will cry out to God Most High, to God who performs all things for me. He shall send from heaven and save me; He reproaches the one who would swallow me up. God shall send forth His mercy and His truth (Psalm 57:1-3).

Psalm 57 and Psalm 142 were written *when David took refuge in the cave because Saul was pursuing him.*

These Psalms were written so that everybody could know why David and his 400 men had taken refuge in the cave.

They are extremely important because they testify how God rescues His children when they call out to Him and trust in Him.

David sang the Word of God, and the Word of God intervened with great effectiveness!

This is still true today. Therefore, let's see how to apply this principle to our personal experiences.

How to Cry Out to the Lord

Psalm 57 leads us directly inside the cave where we observe David and his 400 men turn to God for help.

"I will cry out to God Most High, to God who performs all things for me" (Ps. 57:2). Once again David says, "I will cry out."

Some might object and say that to follow David's example to the letter and cry out to the Lord is a sign of exaltation. However, the reality is that David and his men cried out knowing that God had made a covenant with them.

We have an eternal covenant with God as well; and therefore, it is fundamental to understand its deep implications to be able to cry out and receive what we are entitled to as heirs in Christ![1]

God has bound Himself to each one of us indissolubly and personally, and through this covenant He has undertaken to show His favor toward us. In fact, humankind does not receive anything on the basis of merits and good deeds, but only by *faith* in Him and His love toward us, His children![2]

What is driving you to cry out to the Lord? Whatever situation has brought you inside the cave, you need to know that you can cry out, "Lord, You promised that You will complete the work You started in me!" God will certainly answer. You can be sure that He will intervene in the measure according to your awareness of your position as a child of God.

You have to recognize the importance of crying out to God, and you have to know what to claim in order to receive an answer. Isaiah warns us, "You who put the Lord in remembrance [of His promises], keep not silence, and give Him no rest" (Isa. 62:6-7 AMP). Cry out to God and remind Him of His promises. Praying to God through His promises means reminding ourselves and Him that He has a commitment, and He will keep His word. In fact, God has the necessary power to accomplish whatever He says.[3]

You are still inside the cave, but your heart is starting to change—thanks to faith. Your lifestyle will be transformed, and you will come out of your distress victoriously—thanks to your faith in God the Father.

To Act Means to Put into Practice

We have to learn how *to act* on the promises! Many listen to preachings, recordings, or read books without, however, *translating* what they hear into *practical actions*. They find pleasure in what they have discovered, without *acting*. However, their way of drawing near God is fruitless because listening implies *putting into practice* what one has received, *moving* on the basis of what the Bible says, *acting*, *walking* like Jesus, under the guidance of the Holy Spirit. To act, in fact, does not mean to remain still, but *to walk* by faith.[4]

> *So then faith comes by hearing, and hearing by the word of God* (Romans 10:17).

This is a great truth. However, faith can grow, and its development depends on a life lived in accordance with what you believe on a daily basis.

So if you are in the cave, I encourage you to believe in the Scriptures *with all your heart*, to accept them in full confidence, and to act according to what they say. This is the only way you will be able to see God's hand at work in your situation. You will see God's intervention, and you will testify His delivering power.[5]

Perhaps you are saying right now, "Actually, I have invited God to come inside my cave, but will He really want to enter with me?" Sure He will!

The purpose of this book is to give you this absolute certainty. Without a doubt God always wants to be on your side and in every difficult situation, but it is important to cry out to God knowing how to do so.

The greatness of a problem, the strength of a particular disease, the bills to be paid, and the lack of the money are facts, but they do not have the last word. It is important to fight against your problems by using God's promises, standing firm on His word owing to the *spiritual law* according to which we all reap what we sow.[6] If we sow words of healing, then we will reap the fruits of healing; if with sow unbelief, we will have nothing to reap.

Ask for Revelation with Confidence[7]

The world says that there is only one reality and that it cannot be changed, but as believers we know that reality is not stable and unchangeable as everything and everybody would like for us to believe. Facts can be changed through the vision of what awaits us in Jesus Christ.

Things change when we start to have an inner convincement. God cannot change our situations unless we firmly believe in our hearts that He is able and willing to change them. In fact, this is the most difficult obstacle to overcome, considering our natural tendency to act according to our own decisions before receiving guidance from the Lord.

To this concern, I would like to ask you a question, the answer to which is fundamental: Do you know that Christianity is the only revealed religion? In fact, it is written, "The secret [of the sweet, satisfying companionship] of the Lord have they who fear (revere and worship) Him, and He will show them His covenant and reveal to them its [deep, inner] meaning" (Ps. 25:14 AMP). Let's try to understand what the Scriptures want to say through the verb *reveal*.

One day Jesus asked, "Who do men say that I am?" and again, "But who do you say that I am?" Only Peter answered without hesitation, "You are the Christ, the Son of the living God." So Jesus said these words, "Blessed are you...for flesh and blood has not revealed this to you, but My Father who is in heaven" (see Matthew 16:13-19).

These words easily indicate the importance of receiving personal revelation of the Word directly from God concerning a direct revelation of what we read or what happens to us. It is exactly such revelation that makes us understand what it means to be children. In fact, the authenticity of the relation between the Father and us, His children, consists in this: through an intimate relationship we receive personal answers from the Father that enable us to move in the right direction and to recover.

When you face difficulties, do not hesitate to go to the Father. Ask Him for help because you are His child and heir. You will experience the same answers that David and those 400 men received.

Commit Yourself and Enter through the Narrow Gate

I would like to share an episode of my life to emphasize a very important principle.

My wife and I recently celebrated our twenty-fifth wedding anniversary, and we decided to go on a second honeymoon. We went to Capri where we visited the famous Grotta Azzurra.

By typing the words "grotta azzurra" on any search engine on the Internet, it is possible to find the following description:

> "The interior is suffused with magnificent blue tones. The vault, known as the Duomo Azzurro, has an average height of 7 meters rising to 14 towards the back of the cave. The erosion cavity is approximately 60 meters long and up to 25 meters wide. In order to enter the Grotta Azzurra visitors climb aboard small rowing boats, with a capacity for two, maximum three passengers and, lying on the bottom of the boat, enter the low and narrow mouth of the cave. Entrance to the cave is not possible in the presence of south westerly and mistral winds. The entrance to the Grotta Azzurra is formed by a small natural opening in the rocky wall, roughly 2 meters wide and 2 meters high. The roof of the entrance is situated approximately 1 meter above the level of the sea and, for this reason, passengers are obliged to lie down in the boat whilst passing into the cave. The boatman sets down his oars and maneuvers the boat inside with the aid of a chain attached to the vault of the entrance."[8]

This description highlights a very important aspect: in order to enter the cave, we had to pass through a narrow entrance.

So what is this *narrow gate* for believers? Let's see what the Scriptures say about it:

*Strive to enter through the **narrow gate**, for many, I say to you, will seek to enter and will not be able. When once the Master of the house has risen up and shut the door, and you begin to stand outside and knock at the door, saying, "Lord, Lord, open for us," and He will answer and say to you, "I do not know you, where you are from"* (Luke 13:24-25).

The Gospel says that we have to strive to enter through the narrow gate. Many would like to have everything immediately, forgetting that sowing and reaping require commitment. The same principle is true in the spiritual field: God's power can be manifested only when we do our part.

Jesus said on the cross, "It is finished" (John 19:30). He has done His part, now it is up to you to do yours, which is to believe in what He did so that you can quickly reap the fruits of your faith.

Many will be in the presence of the Lord and will hear Him declare, "I do not know you." So they will knock again saying, "But I went to church, I sang and danced every Sunday, I listened to all sorts of messages!" His statement will remain the same. He will repeat, "I do not know you." Why will Jesus say that He does not know these people? Because they did not pass through the narrow gate.

First of all, we have to recognize what Christ did for us, the sacrifice He bore upon His shoulders. We have to put ourselves aside and recognize what God has done for each one of us! We can pass through the narrow gate only with Jesus in our lives.

Triumph Over Your Enemies!

Caves have always been synonymous of refuge, both for men and animals. Psalm 118:8 says, "It is better to take refuge in the Lord than to trust in humans" and in verse 7 we read, "The Lord is with me; He is my helper. I look in triumph on my enemies" (NIV). When we enter the cave, we take refuge in God, and He delivers us from our enemies.

Enemies are not necessarily physical people. Our enemy could be a disease, poverty, and so on. Christianity reaches every aspect of our lives through truth[9] so that *everybody* can come out of the cave renewed in their minds and in their spirits. It is necessary to spread the Good News, to desire for everybody to know about the sacrifice that Jesus made for us when He went on the cross. Every nation can be delivered only through the Word of God. We need to become *bearers* of the Word of God.

Recognize and Overcome Obstacles

The Grotta Azzurra, mentioned before, was a place for kings. This cave was discovered by Emperor Tiberius who chose it as his private swimming pool. Tiberius already had five villas in Capri, but he had a sixth one built near this wonderful cave in order to bath in its waters every time he wanted. The cave is not a place for poor or religious people. Caves are places for kings.

The Word says that Christ has made us kings and priests.[10] Therefore, the cave becomes the place in which we can become kings, from where we can come out as conquerors, and through which we can make those who live around us overcomers by telling them what we learned while we were inside.

When you enter the Grotta Azzurra, it is dark but when a ray of sun comes in through the narrow entrance hitting the crystal-clear water, the cave is pervaded by a beautiful blue light.

Something similar happens in us when the light of the Word penetrates our critical situations, that is when it enters our personal cave of Adullam. At that point, everything around us is enlightened and shines! Through the revelation of the Word in our hearts, we come out of that refuge as victorious kings.

However, victory belongs only to those who allow God to enter their lives, who follow the guidance of the Holy Spirit and constantly enter into the Lord's presence through prayer, praise, and thanksgiving. In such way, we declare with our mouths and show with our actions that our will is to overcome every obstacle hindering us from seeing God's throne.

The Bible is full of characters who won their battles because they had the courage to face and overcome the obstacles they had in front of them.

Just think of the paralytic man whom the four friends lowered in the house from a hole in the roof just so they could present him to Jesus.[11] The four youngsters were not discouraged by the crowd, but opened a passage in the roof so they could see their friend healed. Think of Bartimaeus who was blind, but when he heard that Jesus was passing by, he overcame the noise of the crowd around him and cried out without minding those who kept on telling him to be quiet.[12]

Let's read another Scripture in John 11:38-39, "Then Jesus, again groaning in Himself, came to the tomb. It was a *cave*, and a stone lay against it. Jesus said, 'Take away the stone.'"

Between Jesus and Lazarus, or actually between Jesus and Lazarus's resurrection, there was an obstacle—a stone. What did Jesus do? He ordered it to be removed. The Word of God is the supreme authority that tells us to remove the stone, and I have chosen to follow its orders. If you have decided to follow the light of the Word as well, let me say something: you will come out of the cave as king and overcomer, just like David and his men.

"Martha, the sister of him who was dead, said to Him, 'Lord, by this time there is a stench, for he has been dead four days.' Jesus said to her, 'Did I not say to you that if you believe you will see the glory of God?'" (John 11:39-40). It does not matter if there are situations in your cave which may seem dead. If you believe, you will see God's glory in your life! God sends His Word and it never returns void without producing changes.[13]

Take Refuge in the Shadow of the Lord[14]

Let's go back to Psalm 57 to highlight another important aspect.

Be merciful to me, O God, be merciful to me! For my soul trusts in You; and in the shadow of Your wings I will make my refuge, until these calamities have passed by. I will cry out to God Most High, to God who performs all things for me. He shall send from heaven and save me; He reproaches the one who would swallow me up. God shall send forth His mercy and His truth (Psalm 57:1-3).

In the midst of his difficulties, David *cried out* to the Almighty and *was sure* that God would deliver him and his men. How could he be so sure? David had this certainty of faith because he had taken refuge under God's wings. So let's analyze what it means to take refuge under someone's wings.

The expression *to take refuge under the wings of a powerful man* indicates someone who offers to protect those who place themselves under him and therefore receive his favors. Where does this expression come from? I believe it derives directly from the Bible.

Just think of the Ark of the Covenant. By observing its representation, you can notice that right above the propitiatory—the lid under which was Aaron's rod, the manna, and the tablets of the Covenant[15]—there were two angels with their wings open, covering everything so that God would not see humanity's sin. Every year, blood was sprinkled on this lid as a sign of the covenant between God and humankind, for the atonement of the people's sins.

Therefore, the expression *to take refuge under the Lord's wings* recalled to David's mind the wide open wings of the angels on the Ark, which indicated the place where God's presence abided. David knew the architecture of the Ark very well, and he knew that those wings represented the place where God manifested Himself in all His power, authority, and glory. David chose to take refuge in God's presence or under His wings, where humankind and God can speak face to face!

We have lost track of that Ark since the day the veil of the temple was torn in two from top to bottom[16] and Jesus died for us. Some believe that the Ark was stolen by Roman soldiers, but I believe that it is in God's presence. In fact, in Revelation 11:19 it is written, "Then the temple of God was opened in heaven, and the ark of His covenant was seen in His temple...." So I believe that the Ark is treasured in heaven.

Today the Presence of the Lord Abides in You

The Ark of the Covenant represented God's presence in the midst of His people; but now that the Ark no longer exists, where can we find God's presence? Where can we pour out our complaint and our desperation? Where can we meet the Lord today?

The answer is very simple: God's presence is in you! Owing to the New Covenant, we no longer need images, statues, or structures to indicate the place where God abides.

Today God's presence is within each one of us! When the Lord wants to communicate with us, He does it through the Holy Spirit who abides permanently within us. Therefore, if you want to talk to God, you will find Him inside you.

The cave of Adullam, which we all need to search and in which we need to take refuge, is in our hearts. This is where God manifests His power, authority, and glory.

Under the New Covenant, it is no longer difficult to carry the Ark because God's presence is always in us. All we need to do is learn how to recognize it and express it in everything we do, wherever we go, in the people we meet, and in the circumstances in which we find ourselves. Wherever we go, we can and have to manifest God's presence in us!

> I will say of the Lord, He is my refuge and my fortress; My God, in Him I will trust. Surely He shall deliver you from the snare of the fowler and from the perilous pestilence (Psalm 91:2-3).

David's words remind us that only by taking refuge in the Lord we can experience real changes in our lives.

David and his 400 men believed in God's intervention and in His desire to save them, and therefore His help did not delay in manifesting itself. Follow their example: believe in your heart and declare your faith with your mouth. This is how you come to witness God's intervention. You are bound to God by a covenant, owing to which you have been delivered from your past bondages and the gates of prison have been opened—you are free!

For sure He will deliver you. God will deliver you. The Scriptures do not say *perhaps*. It is written, *for sure*. God leaves no space for doubt. God is sure of what He promises and has the ability to accomplish every promise.

The right question is rather this: Do you believe in what God said?

Listen to His promise again, "...If they drink anything deadly, it will by no means hurt them; they will lay hands on the sick, and they will recover" (Mark 16:18).

God declared these words, but do you have the inner *certainty* of what He said? He added, "In My name they will cast out demons; they will speak with new tongues" (Mark 16:17).

Once more God says something extraordinary, but do you have the inner *certainty?* Do you really believe it?

Believing in the Word of God is what makes the difference.

Because he has set his love upon Me, therefore I will deliver him; I will set him on high, because he has known My name. He shall call upon Me, and I will answer him; I will be with him in trouble; I will deliver him and honor him. With long life I will satisfy him, and show him My salvation (Psalm 91:14-16).

Chapter Four

A PLACE
FOR RENEWAL

The Cave: A Place for Preparation

The Lord also will be a refuge for the oppressed, a refuge in times of trouble. And those who know Your name will put their trust in You; for You, Lord, have not forsaken those who seek You (Psalm 9:9-10).

In the previous chapter we observed how the cave is a place for kings. Now we will see how the cave of Adullam is in no way whatsoever gloomy, but rather a place for preparation in which a group of people gathers together to grow and become one single body—an organism that moves in harmony for the good of all.

These simple verses in Psalm 9 teach us the fundamental importance of unity in prayer or corporative prayer.[1] In fact, when we take part in a real corporative prayer, we obtain victories as a group! To obtain such victories, it is necessary for the entire group to attend the same school, that is the same local church, the place where we prepare for battle and win together.

Claim Your Victories Today

David and the 400 men entered the cave lacking in everything, but they came out strong and victorious knowing how to destroy giants. They entered defeated and in misery, but they *all* came out so rich that they were able to present great offerings to the Lord!

We will discover what transformed them into mighty men while they were in the cave, their names being mentioned in the Bible.

Do you know that our names are written in the Book of Life?[2]

There is a book in heaven in which all the believers' names are recorded—the Lamb's Book of Life.[3] The book does not contain the names of all humankind, only those of believers. This is good news that should drive us not to be content with the possessions and victories awaiting for us in the future, but should encourage us to live in victory in the present. In fact, in heaven we will have no enemies, there will be no more problems and battles to fight, no more tears, distress, and curses. It is only here on earth that we can make ours the victory which we need *today*!

It is *now* that we are called in Jesus Christ to form an army capable of winning all battles. Tomorrow there will no longer be any need to win battles because we will be immersed in the Lord's presence. He is preparing a wonderful place for us as promised. Therefore, our task is to put into practice every day what the Scriptures teach us in order to make God's promises ours and enter into the victory that we need daily. This is why we absolutely need to understand what happened inside that cave.

The Lord Is Your Refuge

First of all, the cave represents the place in which we take refuge.

For sure a cave is not a noble palace or a luxury building, but it is a safe and protected place in which we gather to be trained and prepared for battle.

The cave in which I received my preparation was the Bible school I attended and for which my family and I had to face several changes. When we left home, we took just what was indispensable for us, leaving many things behind: the city in which we lived, our house, our jobs, our incomes, our family, the church, and the responsibilities my wife and I had in church. In other words, we left all our certainties behind us. Everything ahead of us was uncertain, even if we had made the right decision.

We were determined to invest our time in the Lord and discover what His plans were for us so we could then transmit them to others.

We encountered great difficulties when we entered the school-cave, but when we came out, the Lord had prepared us to be victorious warriors with a heart ready to follow Him.

In Psalm 9:9-10, we learn the spiritual value of a *refuge* for each one of us.

> *The Lord also will be a **refuge** for the oppressed, a **refuge** in times of trouble. And those who know Your name will put their trust in You; for You, Lord, have not forsaken those who seek You* (Psalm 9:9-10).

The Lord is an *inexpugnable* refuge in times of trouble.

There is another verse which I often love to repeat in prayer, "Lord, You are my stronghold and my refuge!"[4]

When we take our children to nursery school, they are still very small and defenseless. However, we know that the nursery is a protected and safe place for them. I like to go back to my "nursery school" every day knowing that it is my stronghold.

But where do we find our real refuge? In the actual building or cave? No. The Lord is our refuge. David said, "The Lord will be a *refuge* for the oppressed, a *refuge* in times of trouble." David had discovered that his true refuge was not in the walls of his house, let alone in those of Saul's royal palace. The only safe place was the Lord!

When in difficulty, he knew exactly where to take refuge. David would always take refuge in the cave, that is the Lord. He would not go to the king or to the pastor or the elders of the church—he took refuge in the Lord.

In church you will find brothers and sisters ready to agree with you in prayer; however, remember that your life does not depend on others, but on the Lord, on the Spirit of God. In fact, He is the One who directs your life. Therefore, in order to grow spiritually, you have to learn how to depend on the Lord and not simply on people of faith.

My desire is to show you how to depend on God and present your requests to Him, for you to learn how to enter into His presence and leave your burdens at His feet. Only the Lord can reveal how to overcome adversities without being crushed by them. He knows how to take care of you—He is your Father!

The Lord Is Your Source

Only Jesus has fullness of love, resources, and grace. He tells you, "I will not leave you nor forsake you" (Josh. 1:5) and, "I am your stronghold and your refuge."

Although my suggestion to go back to nursery school at our age might seem bizarre, I am not at all embarrassed in repeating to the Lord, "I am happy to come back to Your nursery school, Lord, because I need protection in my life; I need Your help because without You I am alone and I can do nothing."

Perhaps you have often admired your pastor's firmness and strength. The secret of that strength is in the time spent in prayer in God's presence. My strength is in God, my help is in God. If someone sees me strong and firm, this depends on the fact that I spend time with God; I attend *His* nursery school every day. God is my strength, my only source is the Lord.

Who or what is your source? A man, a church, an organization? Jesus is your source! Cry out to Him and He will deliver you from every difficulty; He will take you offshore and will help you reach the desired harbor.

David and the 400 men learned this lesson because David had no money, no land, houses, or a job to help them. David's only wealth with which he could enrich those men was God. By entering into the Lord's presence, they had everything they needed.

As the Scriptures remind us, since God gave us the most precious thing He had, His Son Jesus Christ, "How shall He not with Him also freely give us all things?" (Rom. 8:32).

If the Father gave us His best, He will certainly provide for all our needs. We can obtain answers from God by faith in the promises contained in the Word.[5] Every believer has the same rights of a pastor when in God's presence, because we are children of the same Father.[6]

What we have to search for, more than anything else, is a personal revelation of the Word of God that enables us to act on the basis of a heart full of faith. So we enter into His presence and receive everything we need from Him. We can enter into His presence with sure faith and stand in front of the throne of grace because God has *already* provided everything for us in Jesus Christ.

When David entered the cave, he believed in God and in His promises; he spoke and acted on the basis of what God had said. Then the circumstances and his heart started to change.[7]

Let's follow this righteous man's example and set our eyes on God, because He is our refuge.

The Lord Is Your Light

Another characteristic of a cave is darkness. "The Lord is God, and he has made his light shine on us" (Ps. 118:27a NIV).

The cave was not full of light, but in order to see clearly and enlighten the 400 men who had followed him, David did not need natural light as much as he did spiritual light. The Bible says, "The Lord shall enlighten my darkness" (2 Sam. 22:29; Ps. 18:28).

If you need revelation to obtain clarity on matters that you cannot resolve, you need to know how to receive it from God. The Bible says in Proverbs 20:27, "The spirit of a man is the lamp of the Lord."

Your spirit is the means through which God makes His light shine. When you listen, He enlightens your spirit letting you know what to do.

Advice from people is good, but not always in line with God's wisdom; so when you ask a believer to give you advice, be sure he or she is a mature Christian. Do not ask for advice just from anybody, because not everybody has the spiritual maturity to give advice. An immature Christian may give you good advice based on his or her own experience, but not according to the Word of God.

Humankind is composed of three parts: spirit, soul, and body. The body is a sort of shell that behaves like the chassis of a car. Although it might be deformed, the motor keeps working without any problems. The same can happen with our bodies. Even if they are not in perfect condition, this does not prejudice their movement.

The *real you*, the engine of your life, is your spirit. Our essence is our spirits that reflect God's image.

Then, we have a soul—our minds, wills, and emotions together.

Last, we live in a body.

It is the spirit that distinguishes us from animals since this is the part that shows our likeness to God. Man was created in God's image and likeness and in no way whatsoever did we come from monkeys.[8] We are beings created by God's hands!

If owing to your incapability to listen, God were obliged to talk to a donkey, He would have no problems in doing so.[9] God wants to establish a personal relationship with you and therefore communicate and speak directly to your spirit. When you are buried in darkness and need revelation, His Spirit will let you know within you if you are doing the right thing or not. What you have to do is start listening to God with an open and sincere heart.

However, after listening, you will be free to choose. Usually, when you do the wrong thing, you end up accusing whoever gave you advice without taking the responsibility for your actions in front of God. This hinders you from growing. You need to be willing to spend time in God's presence so you can learn how to *discern* His voice.

The Spirit of God is in constant communion and communication with our spirits. Therefore, it is important to listen to what God has to tell us so that our choices may be enlightened. For example, before making any decision, ask the Lord which is the right job for you and do not immediately choose the one that gives you a better income. Only God knows what there is in store for you and can give you the right advice.[10] Once you listen to His voice, everything will depend on your choice—to follow God's advice and therefore be victorious and accomplish your destiny, or to follow your own decisions standing as a candidate for defeat.

The final responsibility is only yours. So when you find yourself in such a situation, you can declare, "This time I will wait in the Lord's presence and allow Him to guide me, and I will do what He says. I will listen and follow God's voice and not what my common sense suggests. I will not be seduced by the voice of money." Money has a voice through which it often shouts out loud, but the Lord's voice is always louder. If you train your ear, you will be able to hear and learn how to discern what is best for you.

David allowed God's light to enlighten his darkness. Only God can enable you to read the events of your life in the light of truth, through His Spirit living in your heart. Every day, your victory will depend on this.

The Cave: A Place for Cleansing

Christianity is very practical: It is better to spend a couple of hours in God's presence and make the right decisions that produce lasting fruits of joy, rather than neglect this brief moment and live the consequences of a wrong choice for years.

The Lord is always willing to help us out of the consequences of our wrong choices. However, His fatherly desire is to help us avoid problems in the whole and not have to help us when we are in difficulty due to our mistakes. As the proverb says, it is better to prevent than to cure.

God Raises You Out of the Dust

Let's continue examining the cave. Usually, it is a dusty place, not at all welcoming or clean. Dust reminds us of the words in Psalm 113:7, "He raises the poor out of the dust, and lifts the needy out of the ash heap."

David entered that cave together with other men knowing that they would have experienced how *God raises the poor out of the dust, and lifts the needy out of the ash heap.*

God knows how to deliver us from dust and mud. Before accepting Jesus as our personal Savior,[11] we lived in the mud of the world, that is in sin. We were created by God; therefore, even if buried in mud, we carry many precious things with us. God knows how to deliver us from the quicksand of sin and how to find the precious gems hidden inside of us!

If you still have not accepted Jesus in your life by saying: "Lord, I accept You as my personal Savior!" you have not been cleansed from *that mud* yet.

There is only one spiritual detergent that can cleanse you—the blood of Jesus. It is the blood of Jesus that purifies us from *every* sin![12] When the blood of Jesus cleanses you, then the mud of the world is washed away and God's blessings can come into your life. From that moment on you will be cleansed and shining, and able to walk with the Lord.[13]

What should believers do when, along their journey, they get dirty again with the mud of sin? Do they have to accept Jesus Christ again as their personal Savior? No! It is sufficient to accept Him once. Do they have to repeat baptism? No, also baptism is received once. When we get dirty with the mud of sin, the Bible tells us that we have to present ourselves to Jesus and recognize our transgressions asking Him to forgive us. Then, His blood cleanses us and we are white as snow again.[14]

David experienced how God raised the poor out of the dust and lifted the needy out of the ash heap. Dust and ash heaps are not where God placed humankind. God placed Adam in the Garden of Eden, a place of blessing in which there was every kind of fruit-bearing plant and animal, a place in which the Bible says God placed gold, silver, and every kind of precious gems so that man could benefit from them.[15] God did not mean for man to live in dust and ash heaps when He created him!

You Are a Precious Jewel

This is really good news for those who still do not know Jesus—humankind was not created to live in dust and ash heaps. Only satan was condemned to crawl and eat dust for eternity. We are called to cover another rank[16] because we are precious in God's sight.

God compares us to precious jewels, diamonds of great value.[17] Each one of us is extremely precious in His sight!

This is how God sees us, which is in stark contrast with how the world sees us. In fact, the world considers a person valuable if he or she is a millionaire living in Hollywood, in a wonderful villa with a swimming pool. These rich people do not count much in God's eyes because if they are not born again[18] they are living in mud, while we are walking in heavenly places in Jesus Christ.[19]

The Word of God helps us renew our minds.[20] What the world considers of value is very often not considered so by us who follow God's path, which is wholly, clean, safe, cleansed by the blood of Jesus and viable only by the righteous. When we accept Jesus, He makes us righteous through salvation, which is something that no riches of this world can buy. In fact, justice is a gift from God.

I can state with certainty that I am righteous because I have been cleansed by the blood of Jesus, the Lamb of God.[21] It is a right you can claim if you have accepted Jesus into your life. Repeat this truth several times until you believe it with all your heart. When the enemy, the adversary, the snake, satan accuses you to deprive you of your blessings,[22] hit him with the truth reminding him of his future: I am righteous, while you are defeated, condemned to eat the dust of the earth all the days of your life (see Genesis 3:14).

Therefore, the cave becomes the place of dust reserved for the enemy and not for God's children. In that spiritual place those men learned how to consider themselves in a new way and declare, "Although we are really discontented, in distress, and in debt, we are justified and we will not stay here forever."

The Word Is Power for Whoever Believes

A typical phenomenon we can experience inside a cave is that of echo. Psalm 119:160 says, "The entirety of Your word is truth, and every one of Your righteous judgments endures forever."

The term *entirety* means that we cannot extract from Scriptures what we are interested in, making the Bible say what it does not say at all.

It is necessary to draw from the totality of the Scriptures and put into practice *everything* it teaches so that our lives in Christ may be true and founded on the Bible. If we desire to become everything it promises, we cannot be satisfied with only part of it, ignoring its whole.

When David spoke in the cave, his voice echoed and was amplified.

We know that the Word of God is power for whoever believes.[23] The Gospel is God's *power* for the salvation of those who believe. And since we believe, when we declare His Word, it is amplified or echoes within us. The Word becomes part of us like food providing energy to our whole body. In fact, the Word of God becomes effective only when it is assimilated.[24]

This was one of the lessons the 400 men learned inside the cave, because it was not sufficient for them to rely on just what David knew. They wanted to learn personally how to exit that place through faith in the Lord.

David was a great example for them. However, we have a greater and perfect example: Jesus! He is our example.

Can man come out of poverty without listening to the Word? Can we make it without meditating on the Word? It is impossible. God invites us to meditate on it to be successful in all our ways and to prosper.[25]

In order to give stability to our lives, we have only two possibilities—either listen to God's voice or the world's. Victory or defeat depend on this choice.

The Bible is the Word of God sealed by the blood of Jesus! It never fails and it is always valid! Wherever the Gospel is proclaimed, transformations occur. Preaching generates faith in those who listen and see in Jesus Christ their anchor of salvation and deliverer. In fact, the power of God comes out of the mouth of those who declare the Gospel! If you are full of the Word, then you are also full of God's power.

The Word is dynamite, which, however, remains ineffective if it is not put in contact with the gunpowder that causes the explosion.

The same is true for us. When the dynamite of the Word is in us, all it takes is for someone to ask us the reason of our faith and, like a fuse, we explode with all the power of the Word!

John 8:31-32 is useful for those who want to receive baptism, "Then Jesus said to those Jews who believed Him, 'If you abide in My word, you are My disciples indeed. And you shall know the truth, and the truth shall make you free.'"

On the basis of Jesus's words, the first step to take in order to become His disciples is baptism in water. However, it is simply the first step. Jesus continued, saying, "If you abide in My word, you are My disciples indeed." Whoever receives baptism is called to walk in His Word!

Sharpen Your Weapons!

The cave in which David and the 400 men took refuge had to be big enough to host them all. However, I wonder what happened when all 401 of them gathered together in that restricted space. They probably pressed against each other, pushed each other, perhaps making some fall, and the atmosphere might have been tense.

Let's read what the Scriptures say in Proverbs 27:17, "As iron sharpens iron, so a man sharpens the countenance of his friend."

When we all gather in a restricted space spending more time together and getting to know each other, we discover each other's defects and shortcomings. By spending time with other believers, your character is molded and your sword sharpened.

I do not know how 401 men managed to live in the same cave, but I know that from that place they came out as very well-*sharpened* weapons.

Probably some did not like the person next to them, but owing to the lack of space, they had to learn how to live together.

We have to learn how to stay close to each other and accept to be sharpened. Living in a restricted environment will inevitably make us clash with other people's views. When this happens, simply remember that God is molding you. This is the only way you will be able to come out of the cave as a warrior and captain of thousands and captain of hundreds.[26]

Bible school is an extraordinary place for preparation where you learn how to use the Word of God like a sharp sword. If you want to learn how to use it, you have to live in a local church.[27]

Anchor Yourself to God's Covenant with You

What made these men strong? There was an element that ensured their success and grants us victory as well. What is this element?

The answer is in Deuteronomy 8:18, "And you shall remember the Lord your *God*, for it is He who gives you power to get wealth, that He may establish His *covenant* which He swore to your fathers, as it is this day."

The assurance of your victory is not represented by a man, by a church, or your pastor, but by the Lord.

Between you and God there is an indissoluble covenant that guarantees your victory.

God established a *covenant* with man when He said to Abraham: "I establish an eternal covenant with you and I will do certain things for you." Through Abraham, God entered a covenant with us. God established an eternal alliance with humankind.

In what does this covenant consist?

> *And I will establish My covenant between Me and you and your descendants after you in their generations, for an everlasting covenant, to be God to you and your descendants after you* (Genesis 17:7).

Since it is an eternal covenant, it extends to me and you as well. So what is this covenant between us and God that gives us the assurance that He will fulfill His promises?

In the Old Testament, two people entered a covenant through the mingling of their blood, which bound them until death. How are you bound in a covenant of blood with God today? Just think of Jesus's wrists and you will see the open wounds out of which His blood poured to establish the new and eternal alliance with us.

The blood of Jesus is what guarantees your victory over difficulties, over debts and problems. The blood that came out of Christ's pierced wrists is the guarantee that we are God's children, bound to Him by means of a covenant through which He promised to take care of us according to all our needs![28]

The moment two people came into an alliance in the Old Testament, they put everything they had in common. The person binding himself to another through a covenant was basically offering his help in every occasion. When one party was assaulted by an enemy, sickness, a debt, or any other difficulty, the other party was called into action.

Since you have entered a covenant with Jesus, He will enter into your problems owing to the blood that binds the two of you together. Jesus was always present in all of the disciples' difficult circumstances. Jesus still tells you today, "I will not leave you nor forsake you" (Josh. 1:5).

THE CAVE: A PLACE FOR THE MIND'S RENEWAL

What does this New Covenant guarantee? Let's read First Corinthians 11:25, "In the same manner He also took the cup after supper, saying, 'This cup is the new covenant in My blood. This do, as often as you drink it, in remembrance of Me.'"

This cup is the sign that we have entered a covenant with God through Jesus.

Every time we take part in the Lord's Supper we remember that covenant. It guarantees that God will provide for us in every circumstance. If we find ourselves in the cave, we can come out as conquerors because we are bound to God by an eternal covenant.

When we believed in Jesus Christ and accepted Him as our personal Savior, we entered an eternal covenant with God owing to which He takes care of our precarious situations and problems, and comes inside the cave with us.

At this point all we have to do is discover what God promised Abraham, which remains valid for us still today.

> *I will make you a great nation; I will bless you and make your name great; and you shall be a blessing* (Genesis 12:2).

Through these words, God promises Abraham (and us, his descendants through the covenant in Christ Jesus) that He will do three things:[29] *I will make you, I will bless you, you shall be.*

"I Will Make You"

The first action that God accomplishes concerns us directly. First of all, He changes us, and then He changes the circumstances around us.

First God changed Abram's name into Abraham,[30] which means *father of a multitude.*[31] Abraham had no children when this took place and therefore no possible descendants. However, God immediately changed his name to *father of a multitude.*

The first thing that had to change in Abraham was his mindset. Abraham considered himself of little value because he had no descendants to whom he could hand down his inheritance.

By changing his name, God modified Abraham's identity. He became a different person compared to what he had been up to then and could therefore inherit the blessings to which God had destined him.

God acts in the same way with us today. He reveals Himself through His biblical promises making us see how He is the Lord our Healer.[32] All we have to do is believe in what He says and confess His Word every day saying, "You are the Lord who heals me!" continuing to prophesy this word until we receive the actual revelation. Once we receive it, we will be able to *really* believe that the Lord heals.

Through faith we come into agreement with the divine promises. The Word of God is deposited in our hearts where it takes root renewing our minds, and divine healing manifests itself. If we do not renew our minds, we cannot make ours the blessings that God has in store for us. Abraham was not wealthy when he received the promise, but he believed without doubting, and through that process he took what God had prepared for him.

Psalm 142:7 says, "Bring my soul out of prison, that I may praise Your name; the righteous shall surround me, for You shall deal bountifully with me."

David *knew* that the Lord was ready to cover him with wealth when he still possessed nothing. He fully believed in God's promises and prophesized His Word in faith. He did not deny his state of poverty and danger, but he believed and confessed the Lord's promises.[33]

"I Will Bless You"

First of all God changes our mindset, putting it in agreement with His Word. If He does not change us first, He will not be able to bless us. In fact, His blessings are at our complete disposal. However, if we cannot first see them through the eyes of faith, we cannot believe in them and it will never be possible for them to be fulfilled in our lives.

It is like being in possession of a winning lottery ticket. If you do not present the ticket to the authorities showing that you won, you cannot cash in the amount that you are owed. In the same way, we have to *learn* how to inherit God's promises and take possession of that inheritance—God said, "I will bless you."

Let's have a look at what the blessing in Genesis 24:1 actually consists of, "Now Abraham was old, well advanced in age; and the Lord had blessed Abraham *in all things.*" Abraham was blessed *in all things*; God wants to bless His people *in all things!*

In all things includes the solutions to all your problems. God is able to provide for all your needs!

This is the blessing declared over Abraham's life, and we inherit it through Jesus! Therefore, we too are blessed *in all things!*

"You Shall Be"

God changes our mindset so that we may be blessed in all things and be a blessing for others.

We need to learn how to make those blessings ours in order to help our neighbor. In fact, no one can give what he or she does not have. Therefore, praying that the Lord may bless us in every area of our lives is not a form of egoism but the only way to bless those around us.

In Genesis 39:2-3 we see how we can become a source of blessing for others:

> *The Lord was with Joseph, and he was a successful man; and he was in the house of his master the Egyptian. And his master saw that the Lord was with him and that the Lord made all he did to prosper in his hand.*

Joseph is another Old Testament character who experienced great difficulties during his life. He served Potiphar, an officer of Pharaoh's, captain of the guard[34] thus with a position of regard. Owing to this position, Potiphar had every kind of wealth: power, riches, and honor. However, he noticed something peculiar in Joseph, and what he saw led him to the conclusion that the Lord was with him. Joseph was an intelligent and wise man; he succeeded in everything he did and everything in his hands prospered.[35]

If Christians are always sick, depressed, in debt, full of problems, and unsatisfied, the world will not be able to notice that the Lord's presence is with them. Believers mistake in saying, "God sent us this sickness, this problem. We can't do anything about it."

Such things do not show the world God's presence in us. It is not God but the enemy who causes sickness and poverty, and all the verses shared up to now confirm this truth.

What drove Potiphar to discern that the Lord was with Joseph? Was it the fact that Joseph was sick or poor? No. He noticed how Joseph prospered in all his ways. For this reason Potiphar said, "The Lord is with him!"

Joseph had been previously cast into a pit by his brothers, but the Lord was with him in that pit and pulled him out of it alive,[36] just like David and the 400 men came out of the cave!

We have to start considering difficulties as opportunities to know God more intimately and to experience how His power transforms us to be *more than conquerors*. This takes place only if we set our eyes on the Word and trust in Him.

God shows His power first by *changing* us and then by *blessing us* in all things so that we may be a *blessing for others*.

God never leaves us in our state of misery because He wants to use us to bless others. However, He will not be able to do so if we continue complaining about everything and everybody. First of all God has to renew us, and only afterward He can use us as examples of the life that awaits those who believe in Him.

Chapter Five

MAKE THE DIVINE
PROMISES YOURS

Accept His Divine Promises

Now David said, "Is there still anyone who is left of the house of Saul, that I may show him kindness for Jonathan's sake?" And there was a servant of the house of Saul whose name was Ziba. So when they had called him to David, the king said to him, "Are you Ziba?" He said, "At your service!" Then the king said, "Is there not still someone of the house of Saul, to whom I may show the kindness of God?" And Ziba said to the king, "There is still a son of Jonathan who is lame in his feet." So the king said to him, "Where is he?" And Ziba said to the king, "Indeed he is in the house of Machir the son of Ammiel, in Lo Debar" (2 Samuel 9:1-4).

I have already mentioned how important it is to set our eyes on God in every circumstance, to cry out to Him and take root in Him and in His promises. Now let's take a further step and discover what our role is, and what we have to do to inherit these promises.

Change Your Self-Image

In order to learn how to make God's promises ours, it is fundamental to understand what took place in the cave.

Let's analyze what happens when a person enters the cave with a wrong self-image, and how it is possible to come out transformed through redemption through an alliance with Christ Jesus.

There is a covenant which binds you indissolubly to Christ after accepting Him as your personal Savior. Through this covenant you can take possession of all that redemption has purchased for you through the blood of Jesus.[1] The price that Jesus paid does not simply have to do with our spiritual renewal, but also with our healing, with our deliverance from any kind of bondage, and with victory in every area of our lives!

The price Jesus paid with His blood provides for all these aspects that we need to know in order to use the Word of God, the sword of the Spirit,[2] and resist the enemy's attacks and overcome him. With this weapon we can make God's promises ours and win the battle. When we are in the cave of difficulties, we need to know that we will not remain there forever, but we will come out to reign. In fact, we are called to reign in this life with Christ.

Each one of us goes through periods inside the cave. However, we are not to be discouraged because we know that God will always show us the way out. Just like those 401 valiant men, we too will make it because our alliance is based on better promises.[3]

Let's read Second Samuel 9:1-4 again:

> Now David said, "Is there still anyone who is left of the house of Saul, that I may show him kindness for Jonathan's sake?" And there was a servant of the house of Saul whose name was Ziba. So when they had called him to David, the king said to him, "Are you Ziba?" He said, "At your service!" Then the king said, "Is there not still someone of the house of Saul, to whom I may show the kindness of God?" And Ziba said to the king, "There is still a son of Jonathan who is lame in his feet." So the king said to him, "Where is he?" And Ziba said to the king, "Indeed he is in the house of Machir the son of Ammiel, in Lo Debar."

God wanted to bless this man, but in order to do so He needed a channel. King David offered himself for this purpose asking if there was anyone to whom he could show kindness.

In that Old Testament context, God used King David. In the New Covenant, God constituted Jesus Christ as our King; therefore, when

God wants to show us kindness today, He works through the King, Jesus Christ.

So who was the man God wanted to bless?

It was Mephibosheth,[4] whose name means *without glory*. Mephibosheth was Jonathan's son, who in turn was King Saul's son; so Mephibosheth was King Saul's grandson. Who would not like to be the son or grandson of a king? To be the son of a king means to have every kind of wealth. This man should have had everything in life, and yet his name was Mephibosheth—he who is without glory.

To be Covered with Glory

Mephibosheth represents man when he lost his glory in the Garden of Eden.

In Eden man was covered with glory. The Bible says that Adam and Eve were naked but they did not see their nakedness[5] because they were *covered* with God's glory! They had not committed sin yet, and so they were covered with God's glory. Sin undressed them of that clothing, leaving them naked. So how can man re-conquer the glory with which he used to be covered? Why is man driven by the desire to seek glory in material possessions? Why do men pursue fame?

Humankind is simply in search of that *something* with which he used to be covered and no longer possesses, but which is given back to him through Jesus. In Him we are newly covered of the lost glory.

Mephibosheth was without fame and without glory, crippled and lame. Thanks to his royal blood he should have faced life walking tall; instead the Scriptures tell us that he walked with difficulty. During his childhood something had happened that prejudiced his entire existence. Fearing for his life, his nurse decided to take him somewhere safe, but while fleeing, the child fell from her arms and became lame.[6]

Perhaps in your walk with Christ you have become lame due to a serious fall, to the point that today you limp in the ways of God and believe that you are without glory. But the glory can simply be blurred by the fall, since you received it as a supernatural gift when Christ came to abide in you.

I have good news for you! God will always offer His comfort every time you decide to stand back up. The King wants His children to be able to walk free from the consequences of past falls. There is a real possibility of redemption, deliverance, and forgiveness for all of today's Mephibosheths!

Besides, we know through Scriptures that Mephibosheth lived in Lo Debar,[7] a deserted area. To live in a deserted area does not offer great possibilities, so Mephibosheth did not have great opportunities to earn a living in a respectable way, and this made his situation even more desperate.

This young man was rather unhappy and unable to reach his destiny, to live with dignity. He was young and should have had great expectations; instead he was without glory, in distress owing to his malformation and rather poor because he lived in an area that offered very few possibilities.

Was he not in the same condition in which David and the 400 men had been? Although he was Jonathan's son and King Saul's grandson, he lived in distress. Why? The Bible answers this question very clearly saying that he was *ignorant*.

This adjective is not to be considered as an offence. The term *ignorant* simply indicates someone who ignores something. Therefore, Mephibosheth ignored some things; in other words, he had no knowledge of them.

Romans 10:1-2 talks about knowledge in the following terms: "Brethren, my heart's desire and prayer to God for Israel is that they may be saved. For I bear them witness that they have a zeal for God, *but not according to knowledge.*"

Israel, the people of God, had zeal but no knowledge. So we can have zeal for the things of God but lack in knowledge. Those who have zeal but no knowledge of the things of God cannot receive His justice and will therefore strive to create their own, or justify themselves.

In this way, humanity always tries, through our own efforts, to accomplish what Jesus has already accomplished for us. This has serious implications. When you are in difficulty, you will resort to your own strength in search for a solution and this will require months or even years to be settled in an uncertain way. Instead, if you rely on divine justice with sincere faith, Jesus will give you the solution, lovingly showing you the way out.[8]

The Scriptures say that through Christ Jesus we have become the justice of God, not on the basis of our own merits, but owing to what Jesus, the King, did for us dying and rising from the dead![9]

God Opens the Doors

If you are looking for clear direction in your life but you still have not found it, make a sound decision today—surrender yourself! Bow down on your knees and seek the King. Go into the Lord's presence and say, "Lord, talk to me and give me revelation because I can't make it on my own!"

The Lord will answer you with these words, "You have finally asked for My help! I have been waiting for you to bow down on your knees in My presence," and immediately a river of revelation will start to flow in your heart. You will feel relieved, and you will know what to do. If you follow what God has revealed to you, the doors that up to today have been closed, will open.[10]

Here is a practical example. Some time ago I took my children to an amusement park. We got on a little train; and during the route, we encountered some doors that suddenly opened in front of us. This is what often happens in life. We do not know how, and yet, since we have started walking in the ways of God, Somebody guides our lives opening the doors in front of our eyes.

To enter the amusement park we had to pay a rather expensive entrance ticket. Once we were inside, I could have exclaimed, "With what we've paid to enter, I'm glad we don't have to also pay to enjoy each of the rides as well—the cost would be exorbitant!"

Actually, the entrance ticket gave us access to all the amusement rides. They all were included in the price. The same is true for salvation, because Jesus has already paid the high entrance price for everybody!

The price Jesus paid represents the entrance ticket to the kingdom of God and it is not limited only to deliverance and forgiveness. In fact, salvation encloses all of God's benefits that are at our disposal without having to pay anything extra.

However, it is necessary to keep in mind that some doors will open as our knowledge of the Word of God increases, as well as our maturity in making decisions with wisdom.

COVER YOURSELF WITH ROYAL CLOTHING

Mephibosheth ignored something very important. "Then Jonathan [King Saul's son] and David made a covenant, because he loved him as his own soul" (1 Sam. 18:3). He ignored that his father Jonathan had made a *covenant* with David!

Let's read verse 4, "And Jonathan took off the robe that was on him and gave it to David, with his armor, even to his sword and his bow and his belt." This act was custom back in David's days when sealing a covenant.

If we further examine these verses, we can notice how, at the moment of the covenant, Jonathan, the king's son, gave David something he owned: he took off his robe. This act indicated the will to put oneself under somebody's protection and pass his blessing onto the life of the one who received the robe.[11]

This story shows us symbolically how God is the Father and the King, while Jesus is the Son. Owing to the King's Son, Jesus, we receive protection and blessing through the blood of the covenant.

Jonathan gave David his clothes, which represent justice. In the same way, we are clothed with the justice of God in Christ Jesus![12]

Through this exchange, David was covered with royal clothing, which is not based on self-righteousness deriving from what we do in our own effort, but it is something we receive as a gift. Just as David received Jonathan's clothing, we receive what Christ accomplished for us and are covered with the clothing of salvation.

In order to seal this covenant, Jonathan did something else; he gave David his sword. Likewise, Jesus put His sword,[13] the Word of God, in our hands. Besides, Jonathan gave his bow. In the Bible we see how bows were the weapons used by Israel against Babylon.[14] In our battle of faith, we have to use our bows with which we can shoot lethal arrows against the enemy.

The Battle of Faith

Faith leads us to the battlefield. From the moment we start praying before God's throne and start claiming the promises to the moment those promises are fulfilled, we will face a period in battle against the enemy who will try to discourage us.[15] If we do not put on the whole armor of God, we will not be able to stand and remain firm against the wiles of the devil (see Ephesians 6:11).

In order to overcome the enemy who wants to steal what belongs to us in Christ Jesus, we need God's justice and grace, the sword of the Spirit, the shield of faith, and the whole armor.

From the moment we present ourselves to God claiming His promises to the moment in which these are fulfilled, we go through what the Bible calls "the battle of faith."[16]

"You Shall Know the Truth..."[17]

Let's go back to First Samuel 18:4: "And Jonathan took off the robe that was on him and gave it to David, with his armor, even to his sword and his bow and his belt."

Last, Jonathan gave his belt. What does the belt represent? Truth.

We need to talk about *truth* in our churches. It is not an abstract concept, but a Person. In John 14:6 Jesus says, "I am the way, the truth, and the life...." If you want to know the Truth, you have to know Jesus and the Word of God.

In these days there is a lot of preaching on love, but we insist little on truth. However, there cannot be a true Christian life if there is no truth. God loves the sinner, but hates sin. Therefore, we have to walk with those who really search the Truth in the Bible.

God said to Joshua, "*This Book* of the Law shall not depart from your mouth, but you shall meditate in it day and night, that you may observe to do according to all that is written in it. For then you will make your way prosperous, and then you will have good success" (Josh. 1:8).

Over and over again the Bible reminds us that *this Book* is never to depart from us. When studying the lives of the great biblical characters, it is clear that these valiant men kept their swords next to them even when they slept. They never separated from their swords. Since you are a warrior of the Lord, it is inadmissible for you to depart from the Word of God at night, which nowadays represents your dark moments of distress.

When you are in the midst of the night and you wake up because urged by God, grab the sword of the Spirit instead of complaining and your circumstances will radically change thanks to this weapon. You will become a strong and valiant warrior who will come out of the cave.

The Scriptures do not say that it was David who brought the 400 men out of the cave. They came out *together* with David, regardless of what David had done for each one of them. Thanks to his example, they found in God the necessary strength to come out as heroes, captains of thousands and captains of hundreds.

You can become a valiant warrior as well, captain of thousands and captain of hundreds, taking off your victim clothes and putting on those of conqueror, and seeing yourself as He sees you.

If you do not enter the school of faith and you do not win your battles, you cannot be a captain and an example for others. In fact, you cannot tell anybody how to come out of the cave if you have not come out yourself. First learn how to come out of the cave with God and then He will make you a real captain.

Claim Your Rights!

Mephibosheth did not know that his father Jonathan had made a covenant with David.

Through that alliance, the two had reciprocally undertaken to defend each other's lives, as well as those of their descendants. However, Mephibosheth totally ignored the existence and the implications of such covenant. Therefore, when Saul and Jonathan died, he fled.

Mephibosheth should have been valiant, but since he ignored the covenant, he hid and lived a miserable life. Instead of walking tall, he lived as a lame man, unable of walking normally and in serious difficulty. He who should have reigned, lived a miserable life in a deserted area inappropriate for the son of a king.

He should have gone to the king and reminded him that he had made a covenant, "You made a covenant with my father according to which I shouldn't be in this miserable condition. You have to help me so that I can recover what has been stolen"![18] However, Mephibosheth ignored his rights and therefore could not claim them.

Knowing that we are God's children, we can present ourselves to the King and claim our privileges given by that position owing to the covenant sealed through the blood of Christ Jesus. This is confirmed by the signs of the nails that are still visible on His wrists today. The scars on Jesus's wrists are the sign of the existing covenant between us and God!

In the Gospel we read that after His resurrection[19] Jesus appeared to Thomas and said, "You are unbelieving? Come here. Put your finger in my wounds and your hand in my side!" When Jesus appeared to His disciples in His resurrected body, the signs of His Passion were still visible.

Those indelible signs manifest the eternal covenant that God made with us, His children. All we have to do is believe in the person and in the work of Jesus and be cleansed by His blood. Those signs give us the right to present ourselves in front of the King and our Lord and claim what the covenant has sealed!

When I was a young student in high school, I was part of a well-integrated class that, for bureaucratic reasons, had to be divided. However, we were very united and we wanted to finish our school year together, so we asked to meet the local education superintendent. Our request was rejected.

The class appointed me spokesperson knowing that I had a high sense of justice that never allowed me accept compromises, and I always wanted the common good. Despite his refusal to meet us, I went to talk to him while my schoolmates waited outside. Our reasons had to be heard. The superintendent's answer was once again negative; actually, he called the police to send us away. I talked with my classmates, and we decided to stop our public protest for everybody's good.

Nevertheless, our determination called the matter to the attention of some teachers who believed in the importance of continuity, so our class stayed together to the end.

During that occasion, we found ourselves like David and his men in the cave. We too were in front of a difficult situation that we faced united, following the way of justice and perseverance, with a captain who knew the group's rights and was ready to move for its well-being. In the end, someone listened.

What are you doing to claim your rights? Are you just sitting and waiting that what you have asked for falls from heaven, or are you standing firm, aware of your dignity and authority as a child of God, claiming the blessings that are already yours in Christ?

What Are Your Covenant Rights?

Let's discover what rights were sanctioned by the covenant through the blood of Christ and are therefore ours.

Now when Mephibosheth the son of Jonathan, the son of Saul, had come to David, he fell on his face and prostrated himself. Then David said, "Mephibosheth?" And he answered, "Here is your servant!" (2 Samuel 9:6)

King David noticed the misery, distress, and poverty of that man, and said: "Mephibosheth."

God knows your name. He perfectly knows your situation and your condition. The King calls you and says, "Mephibosheth! Come here!" He does not accuse you. In fact, God does not accuse anybody. We are God's children, and He has prepared places of honor for us in His kingdom!

The scene between David and Mephibosheth makes me think of Jesus who calls His sheep by name and leads them out. "To him the doorkeeper opens, and the sheep hear his voice; and he calls his own sheep by name and leads them out" (John 10:3).

The King comes and takes us by His hand. How many times has Jesus come and offered us His hand while we have refused His help?

If we really want to be led by Him, we just have to do one thing—stretch out our hand and grab His. It is simple!

The King is always ready to help you, but perhaps way too often He can do nothing because you remain sitting there instead of giving Him your hand that would enable Him to pull you out of the cave you are in.

God always makes the first step toward us, but we have to do our part and meet Him. Instead, we often remain waiting for His hand to come down from heaven like a magic wand.

We are no longer living in the Old Testament era in which the people waited for the manna to come down from heaven. Today we receive everything *through grace by faith!*[20]

God comes and knocks at the door, but He waits for each one of us to open it.[21] When He stretches His hand out toward us, we need to stretch ours out to Him, so that He can grab us and pull us out of the cave.

Be a "Good Steward" of the Grace of God

Let's continue reading Second Samuel chapter 9. In verse 7 we can notice three attitudes: "So David said to him, 'Do not fear, for I will surely show you kindness for Jonathan your father's sake....'" The king intended to show kindness toward Mephibosheth.

What kind of kindness was David talking about? The kindness of God! Let's read verse 3 again: "Is there not still someone of the house of Saul, to whom I may show *the kindness of God?*"

David wanted to show the kindness of God, that is the grace of God.

In First Peter 4:10 we read about the *manifold* grace of God.[22] God's kindness is a *manifold* grace, "As each one has received a gift, minister it to one another, as good stewards of the manifold grace of God."

As believers we often stop at the first form of grace, salvation or spiritual renewal, completely forgetting that grace has different forms. David says: "Don't worry. I intend to show the kindness of God, the manifold grace of God."

Let's continue in verse 7, "I will restore to you all the land of Saul your grandfather."

David wanted to restore to Mephibosheth his *inheritance.* Mephibosheth was the son of a king and had the right to an inheritance that he was not benefiting from for lack of knowledge. David restored it to him.

David represents the figure of Christ who calls us by name and says, "I want to restore your inheritance to you!"

> *Therefore it is of faith that it might be according to grace, so that the promise might be sure to all the seed...and calls those things which do not exist as though they did* (Romans 4:16-17).

The inheritance becomes ours by faith. The inheritance belongs to the children! Since we are God's children, we are not condemned to a miserable life full of difficulties and poverty. When we realize that we are God's children and we know about the covenant with the King—of which Jesus bears the signs—then we *must* recover what belongs to us.

These Scriptures talk about King David, but today our King is Jesus who says to us, "Recover your inheritance. It is already yours and you can recover it by faith!"

The inheritance is at our complete disposal, but we have to take hold of it. We have to do an extremely simple act and stretch out our hand. The Bible says that faith always consists in putting real actions into practice—it talks, it moves, it does not remain seated waiting. Rather, it stands up because faith *"calleth those things which be not as though they were."*

So when, for whatever the reason, you find yourself in the cave of Adullam and you recognize your covenant with Christ because you can still see the indelible signs on His wrists, you have *to act by faith*, that is, *"calleth those things which be not as though they were."*

Perhaps you are sick, but you have to declare what the Bible says, "By Jesus's stripes I am healed!"[23]

In this way your faith starts moving. Sometimes healing will be immediate, while in other circumstances it will not. However, you have to put your faith into practice through the Word, because it is the language that God recognizes. By doing so, you will recover what you were promised through the covenant but was stolen. This is possible because the Bible is a legal document, a will, and as such it is recognized in heaven, on the earth, and under the earth. Nobody can make any opposition to this legal document because when you accepted Jesus in your life, you made a covenant with God.[24]

God's Faithfulness and Love Are Eternal

God will provide for all our needs according to His riches in glory.[25] If you do not know how to pay your debts, present this Bible verse to God. He made a covenant with us and will do what He has promised. He remains faithful even when humankind is unfaithful. The Scriptures say, "He remains faithful,"[26] so when you least expect it and in an unthinkable way, things will change.

"…And you shall eat bread at my table continually" (2 Sam. 9:7). In Revelation 3:20 it is written, "Behold, I stand at the door and knock. If anyone hears My voice and opens the door, I will come in to him and dine with him, and he with Me."

The King wants to dine with us! This verse is often mentioned out of context, as an altar call to accept Jesus as Lord; whereas in this context, Jesus's words are directed to people who are already believers. The Lord says these words to one of the seven churches or *assemblies of believers*.

Jesus knocks at your door because He wants to dine with you at the King's table *every day!* God prepares a table full of delicious food in the presence of your enemies.[27] If you do not sit down and eat what He has prepared, all that abundance will be useless.

This Psalm is an invitation to take a seat at God's table. So get up and go sit at that table! Do not be satisfied simply by the smell of the food on the table. You do not fill your stomach with the smell. You have to open your mouth and eat!

YOUR IMAGE IN CHRIST JESUS

God has prepared a rich table in the presence of our enemies, but it is up to us to sit down and eat, or we will never be satisfied. God expects us to act and make ours what Jesus paid at a high price with His own life for each one of us!

Let's continue reading in Second Samuel 9:8: "[Mephibosheth] he bowed himself, and said, 'What is your servant, that you should look upon such a dead dog as I?'"

Mephibosheth considered himself a dead dog, as we too may often consider ourselves. But the truth is completely the opposite.

We have made a covenant with Christ Jesus and we have to stop considering ourselves as dead dogs or failures. We have to raise our eyes toward the wounds and stripes on Christ's body, which remind us of the covenant. Let's claim our rights as children of the covenant!

The Lord is preparing a wonderful place for us paved with gold, where everything shines with glory and where we will live for eternity.[28]

This is beautiful, but what do we do in the meantime?

The Lord said, "The thief does not come except to steal, and to kill, and to destroy. I have come that they may have life, and that they may have it more abundantly" (John 10:10).

How do we intend to enter into the King's presence? Begging? Or saying, "I am Your son. By accepting Jesus into my life I entered the covenant. Thank You, Lord, because through Your manifold grace I receive grace upon grace."

Start claiming what you need: finances, healing, a job, a wife, a husband, a family, *everything!* Stop striving and come out of your cave.

Start believing in the covenant you have established with Jesus. Not only does it guarantee eternal life, but also daily salvation in your present life.

Despite his royal birth, Mephibosheth considered himself a failure. Therefore, the first thing we have to do is change our self-image. We are a royal people, we have been called to walk tall, to fight in the front line against giants, to command the mountains to move.[29] If we continue considering ourselves as failures, we will end up being content with a dog's bed, while God calls us to live in a palace.

What has to change so that you can come out of the cave you are in at the moment? You have to change your self-image and start seeing yourself with God's eyes. This is the only way you will find the strength to come out of the cave! I consider myself a son of the King, justified, cleansed by His blood, covered with a royal robe. I live my life with the strength He gives me, with the weapons God gave me, with His sword, with the belt of truth, and the awareness of having a covenant with God.

What difference is there between me writing and you reading? What difference is there between a Christian who receives answers from God and one who does not? None! God has made the same covenant in Christ Jesus with both types of believers. You are under the same covenant. You too have the right to overcome because Jesus has paid the same ransom for all. Christ paid the price for all humanity!

Whoever Believes, Receives

The Bible says that Jesus paid for all humanity; however, not all humanity is saved. Jesus paid so that we could prosper in all our ways, but not everybody prospers. Why? Because not everybody believes.

God is not the one who has to change. We are the ones who need to undergo a radical change. From now on, you are no longer to present yourself in front of your King as a dead dog, but as a child, with all your royalty, dignity, and value that are fit for a son or daughter of God.

Mephibosheth was the son of a king despite the fact he was crippled and living in bad conditions. Likewise, we are the King's children despite our weaknesses, mistakes, falls, and sins.

Let's read Second Samuel 9:9, "And the king called to Ziba, Saul's servant, and said to him, 'I have given to your master's son all that belonged to Saul and to all his house.'"

With this order, Mephibosheth inherited all that had belonged to King Saul.

Besides, verse 10 says, "'You therefore [Ziba], and your sons and your servants, shall work the land for him, and you shall bring in the harvest, that your master's son may have food to eat. But Mephibosheth your master's son shall eat bread at my table always.' Now Ziba had fifteen sons and twenty servants."

Mephibosheth came into possession of great wealth, even of Saul's servants. In an instant he had thirty-five people working for him. Is this not prosperity? Until that moment he had lived in Lo Debar, in defeat, desolation, and depression. David sent for him, and when Mephibosheth presented himself, David called him by name and gave him prosperity. Through David, Mephibosheth found his destiny.

Let's read what the Scriptures say in verse 11, "'Then Ziba said to the king, 'According to all that my lord the king has commanded his servant, so will your servant do.'" Mephibosheth ate at the king's table as *son of the king*.

In Christ Jesus we are children of the King of kings and of the Lord of lords, heirs of God and coheirs of Christ. We have the *right* to eat at the King's table *every day as His children*.

Chapter Six

DRAW PASSION FROM YOUR SORROW

by Pastor Chiara Scannapieco

Dear reader, knowing that my wife Chiara's love and wisdom would certainly enrich this book, I asked her to write this chapter. Page after page, you will see how her view is in agreement with what you have read up to now, and your soul will be strengthened by her words. We took on this common commitment, praying that you may come into possession of what God has in store for your life.

Set Your Eyes on God

Who has believed our report? And to whom has the arm of the Lord been revealed? For He shall grow up before Him as a tender plant, and as a root out of dry ground. He has no form or comeliness; and when we see Him, there is no beauty that we should desire Him. He is despised and rejected by men, a Man of sorrows and acquainted with grief. And we hid, as it were, our faces from Him; He was despised, and we did not esteem Him (Isaiah 53:1-3).

The Bible dedicates only two paragraphs to the 400 men who entered the cave in a state of great distress, without ever mentioning what took place inside them. We just know that they entered as losers and came out as conquerors. How long did they stay in the cave? How long did it take for their transformation to take place? The Bible says nothing in regard to those questions.

The previous chapter, Make the Divine Promises Yours, emphasized the importance of maintaining a solid and constant faith while waiting for our prayers to be answered. Now we will examine what to do while waiting so that our faith may remain alive and rooted in God's will.

Your Aim Is God

At a certain point, a prophet went to David and told him to come out of the cave. David obeyed the prophet's word and came out with his men.[1]

Although the Bible does not give us any information concerning what happened in those men's hearts, we can deduct such information by observing what they were like when they came out of the cave. They had drawn a renewed zeal from their distress. Thanks to their experience inside the cave, they came out victorious, having learned from that experience, which transformed them into valiant warriors for the rest of their lives.

The title of this chapter is Draw Passion from Your Sorrow, because *to draw* means to take something from one place to another, or to take out, to extract the essence.[2]

Therefore, to draw means to make the decision to move something from one place to another, orienting it toward a desired point. In other words, it means to have an aim, to take something from its current position to the desired one. Such action is defined and not casual, so it is possible to learn how to draw passion from your sorrow. It is important not to discredit anything from an experience, but to draw or learn from all our situations.

Jesus experienced sorrow and distress, and nobody can understand us better than Him:

> *For He shall grow up before Him as a tender plant, and as a root out of dry ground. He has no form or comeliness; and when we see Him, there is no beauty that we should desire Him. He is despised and rejected by men, a Man of sorrows and acquainted with grief...* (Isaiah 53:2-3).

Besides, God has passion. In the book of Hosea, God spoke prophetically. Often, when the Lord talked to His prophets, He asked them to do something that would visibly transfer into actions what He wanted to say. He asked Ezekiel to lie on his side for 390 days. Every day equaled to a year. This action indicated that His people would have remained captive for 390 years as a consequence of their iniquities. Ezekiel's physical action showed the people how God would have acted toward them. The prophet obeyed; and when the set days finished, God told him to turn over on his other side and to remain lying for another 40 days. This was a visible representation of what would happen to the people if they did not repent.[3]

God ordered His prophet Hosea, "Go, take yourself a wife of harlotry and children of harlotry, for the land has committed great harlotry by departing from the Lord" (Hos. 1:2). Such an order was intended to communicate God's feelings to the prophet and the people.

Hosea said, "Then the Lord said to me, 'Go again, love a woman who is loved by a lover and is committing adultery, just like the love of the Lord for the children of Israel, who look to other gods and love the raisin cakes of the pagans'" (Hos. 3:1).

God wanted to convey His passion to Hosea. When God speaks, He communicates real passion. The lives of many prophets like Isaiah, Jeremiah, Hosea, or Daniel were literally consumed by their passion for the message that God had put in their hearts.[4] Jeremiah said, "There is a fire burning in my bones."[5]

God put burning messages in those men's hearts and they were compelled to speak. It was impossible for them to remain silent!

God Burns with Passion for You

By asking Hosea to obey and marry a harlot, God's message remained alive in the prophet's heart and experience. He thus was able to understand what it meant to love a people who prostituted in front of idols, and what it meant to remain faithful to those who had forgotten about Him by becoming unfaithful.

Although God continued to love Israel with all His heart, the people preferred idolatry.

God used Hosea's life and experience to make the prophet's message alive and *compassionate*.[6] For this reason I use the expression *draw or take out passion from your sorrow.*

In fact, God Himself drew passion from His sorrow. When in the beginning Adam and Eve sinned, God suffered!

Adam and Eve suffered owing to their separation from God, but God suffered from the loss of fellowship with them as well. Since God created man to have communion with him, there was a great sufferance in His heart. However, He did not lose time feeling sorry for Himself saying, "Adam! After all I did for you, you betrayed Me! Poor Me!" Instead, He drew passion from this experience of deep sorrow and made the decision to incarnate Himself and bear our sorrow on Himself. His passion drove Him to give Himself for us!

When we are moved by passion, we are willing to face sacrifice in order to see real fruit. Our passion translates into actions. Those moved by passion are able to do great things.

If there is no passion in what you do, you will not be interested in the results. Whereas, when you put all of yourself into what you do, without sparing yourself, you will obtain results that others will notice as well.

God received much fruit from His great passion. His sorrow became passion!

We can see another example of this in birth. When a woman gives birth to a child, her labor pains are transformed into great passion— unlimited love toward a small human being coming from her womb.

The book of Chronicles gives us an excellent example concerning this aspect. After a long and difficult labor, a woman gave birth to a son. The Scriptures say that this son, Jabez, due to his mother's passion and sorrow in giving him birth, obtained more respect than anybody else.

The book presents a long genealogy of names of the house of Judah. However, it specifically talks about Jabez who was the only one who searched God to obtain blessing and deliverance from his fears. And God answered His requests.[7]

Passion Changes Your Life

All your sorrowful experiences should never be sterile or an end in themselves, but should produce results.

Jesus never promised that we would be exempted from sorrows, tribulations, and difficulties. We all have tribulations in this world. However, Jesus promised that He would help us overcome difficulties transforming us into *more than conquerors*.[8]

You can be more than a conqueror treasuring your negative experiences. And the treasure is the passion you draw from those experiences. In Romans 9:2, Paul said, "I have great sorrow and continual grief in my heart."

Paul had persecuted the Church. He had killed Christians convinced of doing what was right in God's sight.[9] When Paul had a vision along the road to Damascus, he was converted and convinced of his wrongdoings.

Paul, the man who made so many mistakes and approved with his presence the killing of Stephen, the first martyr of the Church,[10] could have lived persecuted by guilt feelings. However, it was not so, and for God's grace He drew passion from his sorrowful experiences.

Paul's sufferance was terrible when he heard the Lord say, "Saul, Saul, why are you persecuting Me?"[11]

If we think of our lives before our conversions, I am convinced that we all feel sorrow for the wrong things we did when we still lived in ignorance.[12] When we heard the Good News of the Gospel, we were pervaded by the fear of God[13] together with sorrow for what we had done in the past, which drove us to our conversion. How do we respond to this sorrow? Let's follow Paul's example according to what he says in Romans 9:2-3, "I have great sorrow and continual grief in my heart. For I could wish that I myself were accursed from Christ for my brethren, my countrymen according to the flesh."[14]

Paul did not remain still in his sorrow for his past mistakes, but overcame it embracing a sincere passion for all those who did not know Christ and His great love.

The book of Ecclesiastes says that knowledge and wisdom entail sorrow,[15] not because there is something wrong in them, but because when we do not know something, we totally ignore it. Whereas, when we know about it, it can cause us sorrow. In fact, not everything we discover is pleasant.

If you do not turn the television on, you will not know how many people died in the world or in your city. But when you follow the news, you come to know about the sufferance in the world, and that sufferance becomes yours as well. However, if the sorrow remains a simple, "Have you heard what happened?" and does not translate into prayer, it will be sterile, lacking passion.

All those who took refuge in the cave of Adullam entered with sorrow and distress, but they learned something and came out with passion to follow their captain David, the future king of Israel.

We cannot stop in front of sorrow; we have to continue drawing a real passion from it that will empower us to act.

Rejoice in Your Father's Presence

As already mentioned, Jesus experienced sufferance and sorrow,[16] and therefore is perfectly able to sympathize with what we experience in our lives.

Let's read John 16:21-22:

> A woman, when she is in labor, has sorrow because her hour has come; but as soon as she has given birth to the child, she no longer remembers the anguish, for joy that a human being has been born into the world. Therefore you now have sorrow; but I will see you again and your heart will rejoice, and your joy no one will take from you.

In this verse, Jesus was talking to His disciples to whom He had preannounced His imminent death; the disciples were in great distress.

While talking, Jesus saw them sadden, so He added that *nobody* would have taken their joy away from them. Even in the moment of greatest sufferance they would have had an ineffable joy that would have supported them.[17]

Nobody can take your joy away from you. When you come out of your cave, you will know that nobody will ever be able to steal from you what you have learned in your Father's presence!

When we learn what it means to rejoice in the Lord, *always and no matter what*, nobody will ever be able to steal such joy from us. However, if our joy depends on our circumstances, then it will vanish like dew as soon as our circumstances change.

Our joy comes from our relationship with the Lord who is always in us; and therefore, we can rejoice even when we are in sorrow. Nothing and nobody will ever be able to deprive us of such joy.

To Answer God's Calling, We Must Feel Free

Let's go back to the cave of Adullam and observe what David did as soon as he came out.

The Scriptures say that when he went in, his mother and his brothers joined him.[18]

> *Then David went from there to Mizpah of Moab; and he said to the king of Moab, "Please let my father and mother come here with you, till I know what God will do for me"* (1 Samuel 22:3).

The first thing David did when he came out of the cave was to take his father and mother somewhere else. David took care of his parents to the point of saying, "I will take them in that place, until I know what God is going to do for me."

Perhaps David took them to another place because often parents think they know what is best and end up influencing their children's decisions.

I do not refer to the ordinary things of life, but in particular to the relationship with God. Parents can be a real restraint for those who have a particular calling from God.

I do not mean that parents' concerns are something wrong, but in the presence of a calling from God, the sorrow for the separation from a child hinders the ability to draw the necessary passion for spiritual choices. It is important to be able to transform your sorrow into joy without sinking into worries, especially when a son or daughter sets out on the way indicated by the Lord. In fact, if we have passion for God, then He will answer our prayers and support our children.

Sometimes the opposite occurs and parents urge their children to have passion for God. This inner spur has to come from the Spirit, and a parent can only pray until God answers. Only the Holy Spirit convinces the hearts, not the words of a father or mother.

David knew that it was right to take care of his family, but his family was not to hinder him from serving the Lord. Such principle is valid for all those who have relatives or friends who try in every way possible to lead them astray from the ways of God.

If you are in a similar situation, present it to God in prayer and this restraint will lose its grip on you. Accomplish the will of God, whatever it costs, and He will take care of your loved ones. Like David, present people to the King of kings and Lord of lords saying, "You take care of them!"

Your life belongs only to God. It is not a matter of rebellion toward parents, but of dependence on God. You need to learn how to respect your family, but at the same time to say "No!" when it is right to do so.

After cutting the umbilical cord in order to follow God, what should you do in front of the first obstacle? Run back home to mommy and daddy? No. Facing your difficulties is the only way you can show that you have decided to draw a real passion for God from your sorrow and depend on Him.

Run to God! He will answer. We have to learn how to trust in His help and expect Him to answer our prayers.

CUT OFF DEAD BRANCHES AND PROSPER

Another aspect David learned in the cave is never to leave situations unsolved.

When fleeing from Saul, David went to the priest asking for bread. On that occasion, he met a man,[19] Doeg the Edomite, who became a thorn in his flesh.

When Saul discovered that the priest had helped David by giving him food, he told Doeg the Edomite to kill the priest and the Levites. Saul had 85 people killed[20] who were not his enemies, but priests of the very same God who had called him and consecrated him king.

Envy had clouded Saul's mind to the point that he committed an abomination, killing men consecrated to the house of the Lord. Owing to pride, he actually violated God's grace that had called him, blessed him, and placed him as king over the people.

David was informed of what had happened by one of the men who had managed to flee. How did David feel? Here is the answer, "I knew that day, when Doeg the Edomite was there, that he would surely tell Saul. I have caused the death of all the persons of your father's house" (1 Sam. 22:22).

More than 80 people died because David had asked for food for himself and his men.

Guilt feelings generate terrible distress. "How can I live with this guilt feeling? What will I do?"

Once more David teaches us something he learned in the cave: God redeems us and forgives us! David brought to the cave the priest who had survived, and he drew the right passion from his sorrow. From that moment on, the group of fugitives pursued by Saul had their priest and ephod[21]—*God's presence*. Now David could consult the Lord for every step he took.

What do you do when you find yourself in a moment of sorrow like David? Do you search for revenge, are you critical toward others, or do you search for God's presence asking: "Lord, what is the right thing to do? In Your presence I find relief, refuge, comfort, and You know what I should do in this situation, so please tell me."

Will you give space to your own will, your spirit of envy and your pride, or like David, will you grow closer to God making that sorrow your passion?

Until that moment, David had gone to Gad, the prophet, to know what to do.[22] From that moment on, though, David was able to consult God's opinion directly because he had the actual presence of God with him.

David's thoughts were most probably, "I sowed death and desperation because of an innocent act. Eighty-five men died and it was my fault. I cannot continue crying about what has happened. What can I do now? What can I learn from this situation? What is the solution? The solution is God and I will let Him guide me ever more."

Be Delivered from All Burdens

David learned many things in the cave. He showed his men how to reject personal revenge, prefer God's guidance, and grow in intimacy with Him. David had underestimated Doeg the Edomite. However, from this episode he learned a great truth—never leave unsolved situations which could come against you in the future. David learned not to spare anybody.

Let's read First Samuel 27:11, "David would save neither man nor woman alive, to bring news to Gath, saying, Lest they should inform on us, saying, 'Thus David did.' And thus was his behavior all the time he dwelt in the country of the Philistines." David had understood how important it was to cut away things that tied him to the past. Sometimes it is necessary to make cuts, because certain situations can turn against us accusing us.

In Numbers 33:55 God says to His people, "But if you do not drive out the inhabitants of the land from before you, then it shall be that those whom you let remain shall be irritants in your eyes and thorns in your sides, and they shall harass you in the land where you dwell."

Unsolved situations or wrong evaluations can actually hinder growth.

Therefore, I encourage you not to allow wrong things to abide in you. Stop playing around with your life! Deliver yourself from what you recognize as bad. Do not be indulgent toward yourself and toward what in your eyes seems just a little sin or a simple shortcoming. Watch over yourself so that the little things of today do not become giants tomorrow.

Do not search for comprehension from those who do not follow the ways of the Lord. Remember that the ways of God are foolishness for men.[23] Learn to draw passion from your negative experiences, otherwise you will live paralyzed and burdened by guilt feelings.

When my husband and I decided to attend Bible school, we were obliged to leave everything and everybody behind us. We felt an enormous weight for the responsibility of our choice, which also involved our daughters who were totally unaware of the sacrifices attending them. However, we learned how to draw passion from the many uncertainties, presenting our concerns to God who delivered us from every doubt.

Today we would do everything over again with great joy, because in that period we were overwhelmed by the blessing that God showed us in a thousand different ways, also through people to us unknown. God's hand never failed to manifest itself in our family. We gave no space to distractions and set our eyes totally on God and on the things He was showing us, like the value of a family willing to move as a team to serve God and His Word.

Be delivered from all burdens, forgive yourself and others, and allow God's justice to take care of everything. Open your heart; love and listen to the words of the Lord of lords and King of kings. You will move toward a higher level where you will receive all that the Lord desires to pour into your life.

Do not allow your personal will to block you, making you hold on to minor things, depriving you of the best that God has in store for you and hindering you from reaching your destiny. Pull down the barriers you have built, and you will be free to see and touch with your hand our Father's immense goodness and kindness!

Be Firm—Let the Lord Guide You

Is this not David, of whom they sang to one another in dances, saying: "Saul has slain his thousands, and David his ten thousands?" Then Achish called David and said to him, "Surely, as the Lord lives, you have been upright, and your going out and your coming in with me in the army is good in my sight. For to this day I have not found evil in you since the day of your coming to me. Nevertheless the lords do not favor you. Therefore return now, and go in peace, that you may not displease the lords of the Philistines." So David said to Achish, "But what have I done? And to this day what have you found in your servant as long as I have been with you, that I may not go and fight against the enemies of my lord the king?" Then Achish answered and said to David, "I know that you are as good in my sight as an angel of God; nevertheless the princes of the Philistines have said, 'He shall not go up with us to the battle'" (1 Samuel 29:5-9).

Let's examine what David learned in the school of faith after leaving his camp and going with his men to the land of the Philistines.

The Philistines decided to declare war on Israel. David offered to fight by their side, but the captain of the Philistines did not agree because, being Israelites, they could have turned into enemies on the battlefield. The captain of the Philistines, therefore, decided to send David and his men back to their camp where they made a bitter discovery—their wives, children, and everything they possessed were no longer there because the Amalekites had taken everything away. All of David's men lifted up their voices and wept.[24]

Suddenly David felt anguished and in serious danger in front of an army of valorous men. His men wanted to stone him giving him all the fault for the great loss.

Let's read First Samuel 30:3-4, "So David and his men came to the city, and there it was, burned with fire; and their wives, their sons, and their daughters had been taken captive. Then David and the people who were with him lifted up their voices and wept, until they had no more power to weep." David had undergone his men's same loss. He had lost his wife and children, and he cried just as desperately. But then "David strengthened himself in the Lord" and asked God, "Shall I pursue this troop? Shall I overtake them?" (1 Sam. 30:8).

Through this trial, David developed his *character*. In fact, the first thing the cave molds is your character. Faith alone is not sufficient. You need character as well. David was in front of 600 men who were accusing him and wanted to stone him. What did he decide to do? He searched for strength in the Lord and consulted God to know what to do in that new and terrible situation. Then he gathered his men and they all set out to recover what had been stolen, because God had ensured, "Pursue [the troop], for you shall surely overtake them and without fail recover all" (1 Sam. 30:8).

David's attitude was not, "Ungrateful people! I gave you hospitality and protected you, and what do you do? Is this how you thank me? For one single mistake you want to stone me?" He would have had every right to react this way, but he did not.

On the contrary, David continued to show his character. They left as a group of 600 to recover their possessions; but along the road, 200 decided to stop because they were tired. The 400 who continued with David freed not only their wives, children, and possessions, but also those of whom had stopped along the way. When time came to return all that they had recovered, the *"wicked and worthless men"* said among themselves, "…Because they did not go with us, we will not give them any of the spoil that we have recovered, except for every man's wife and children, that they may lead them away and depart!" (1 Sam. 30:22).

Although David had just risked being stoned and he was in their same battle conditions, he said, "My brethren, you shall not do so with what the Lord has given us, who has preserved us and delivered into our hand the troop that came against us. For who will heed you in this matter? But as his part is who goes down to the battle, so shall his part be who stays by the supplies; they shall share alike. So it was, from that day forward; he made it a statute and an ordinance for Israel to this day" (1 Sam. 30:23-25).

David was a man after God's heart, always ready to follow God's will in every situation. He knew what pleased the Lord. His character gave him the ability to influence an entire nation. He was always able to show gentleness despite everything, because he was always willing to learn lessons from which he drew passion. He did not allow words to offend him, but talked to God saying, "Lord, I have You!"

The same is valid for each one of us today. If we do not develop character, we are candidates for inevitable defeat. The kind of *character* I am talking about is not that according to the world, which contemplates overbearing manners, imposing itself at any cost and with any means. I am referring to the capability of answering without irritation when you are accused unfairly, reflecting on your circumstances and drawing passion from the events of life.

This is the only way we can become more than conquerors. Nothing will be able to stop us because evil will not find space in our hearts. No fiery darts sent against us by the evil one will be able to harm us, if we are wearing the breastplate of righteousness, which progressively becomes ours through the renewal of our minds.

Without character, you will not go very far. Sooner or later someone will lay a snare and you will fall. Character is fundamental. If you really want to become a guide, you necessarily need to develop character. We all are tested when we confront ourselves with other people. In fact, things do not always go the way we would like them to go. Sometimes we receive offensive answers or our love is refused. We can choose to be careful with how we react or we can prepare a nice speech to stick to our rights.

God's grace can give you many gifts with which you can bless others. However, character does not depend on grace. You are the one who makes choices. To choose always implies allowing yourself to be transformed by grace, because grace is the divine influence that acts within us, leading us to changes.

Grace, or divine help, is given to all believers, but the responsibility to enable it to grow and work in our lives is up to us. If the tree trunk is not strong enough, the branches weighted by the fruit will break. Without a firm character, sooner or later your branches will break and crush you, and your fall will involve others as well. In fact, your fruit will fall on the ground hitting those under you.

David could have been full of fear owing to Saul's continuous and unceasing persecution. He could have had revenge feelings and say, "Saul, you know that I had the opportunity to kill you twice, but I spared your life.[25] And instead of being thankful, you pay me back with a ruthless pursuit?" David was not the kind of man who reasoned according to these schemes. This is why God chose him instead of others. David was a man after God's heart, who in every circumstance knew how to *draw passion from bad situations*.

Saul was the means through which David developed perseverance, self-control,[26] integrity,[27] ability to follow God's indications,[28] and the fact of being a model.[29] David transmitted these qualities to his men. His way of acting influenced the behavior of more than 400 people to the point that they came out of the cave as valiant captains of thousands and captains of hundreds. They saw with their own eyes the living example of what was the right thing to do, which is to put into practice the Word of God in every situation.

Such attitude enables us to walk in victory, free from envy and feelings of revenge, armed of forgiveness in the mouth and heart, and with faith in God's grace. It is grace that gives us the ability to do what we would never be able to do with the sole help of our own strength.

Develop a character that is pleasing to God! He will never leave you, especially in difficult moments. If you have passion and you show it, you will leave a deep sign in this society and influence others.

Nobody will be able to forget your example of being someone who clenches to God and listens to and follows His voice, not allowing difficulties to harden your heart.

Chapter Seven

THE GREAT BLESSING

BE A MAN OR WOMAN OF GOD

I waited patiently for the Lord; and He inclined to me, and heard my cry. He also brought me up out of a horrible pit, out of the miry clay, and set my feet upon a rock, and established my steps (Psalm 40:1-2).

The cave of Adullam is an important school for all of us. It is a refuge for those who have lost everything. Because of Saul's persecution, David was obliged to flee and leave everything behind him without knowing where to go or what to do. He entered the cave lacking in every kind of possession and human support. So he set his eyes on the Lord and 400 men gathered around him.

In this chapter we will focus our attention on these men in great distress. They represent the means that God uses to accomplish His projects in our favor.

Keep Your Eyes Set on God

The 400 men *"were in distress, in debt, and discontented."* Although they were in misery, they did not lose their dignity, and therefore they were able to support God's project.

What happened in the cave? What transformed those men? We know that David was a man after God's heart. He faced several giants in his life, but God was always with him.[1] God made him strong and firm owing to his unshakable faith. David himself declared not to have ever taken his eyes off of God, in spite of everything.[2] Even in the darkness of a cave, David raised his eyes toward the Lord. He was overwhelmed by problems, but this did not hinder him from keeping his eyes on God. Even when face to face with a giant, he was able to look at God and His promises. Owing to this strength, which he conveyed to his men, David was able to overcome.

When they came out of the cave, David and his men went to Mizpah.[3] What does this place represent? Mizpah was a place of blessing where Jacob had established a covenant with Laban.[4] Therefore, Mizpah is the place of the covenant.

We too are in an eternal covenant with Christ Jesus. This covenant establishes God's commitment toward us. He has committed to take care of our salvation and all of our needs. This covenant guarantees not only our future eternal life, but also our present life, having become children of God through the blood of the Lamb. This blood gives us the assurance that God will help His children!

The Privilege of Being a Child of God

God always helps His children, but are we all God's children? The Bible teaches us that this is not so. We all are God's creatures, but we all are not His children. In order to become His children we have to be born again, accepting Jesus as our personal Savior. Through this new birth, we enter into a relationship[5] with God.

When we are born again, we become part of God's family. Here is how Jesus explained to Nicodemus how to enter the Kingdom of God: "You are a devout observant of the Law, a religious man, you go to church, give your offerings, help those who are in need, but if you are not born again you cannot enter the Kingdom of God." And Nicodemus asked: "What do I have to do? Do I have to enter my mother's womb again?" And Jesus answered, "To be born again you need to be born of water and spirit."[6]

The water referred to by Jesus symbolizes the Word of God that is to be preached. Whereas the human "spirit" is dead because of sin; it has to be born again or be risen. In hearing these words, Nicodemus's eyes were opened.

He studied and knew the Law and had a certain preparation in the things of God, but he did not have a living relationship with Him. He ignored the richness of the spiritual renewal linked to the new birth that Jesus was presenting him with absolute simplicity.

How to Inherit God's Blessings

Let's go back to Jacob and the town of Mizpah, the place of the covenant. Jacob had a peculiar character. He was a supplanter, a person shrewd in deceiving people. However, he had fundamental characteristics: he feared God, he knew His blessings, and he did all he could to inherit them. Let's have a look at three specific episodes concerning Jacob.

The first episode is in Genesis 31:45-49:

> So Jacob took a stone and set it up as a pillar. Then Jacob said to his brethren, "Gather stones." And they took stones and made a heap, and they ate there on the heap. Laban called it Jegar Sahadutha, but Jacob called it Galeed. And Laban said, "This heap is a witness between you and me this day. Therefore its name was called Galeed, also Mizpah…."

Mizpah was a place of blessing that marked Jacob's life. This is the place where he made a covenant with his father-in-law Laban, on the basis of Laban's words, "May the Lord watch between you and me when we are absent one from another…God is witness between you and me!" (Gen. 31:49-50).

In Genesis chapter 25 we discover that Jacob tried to take possession of his brother Esau's blessing. Since Esau was the eldest son, he had the right to his father's inheritance.[7] The Scriptures say, however, that from his birth Jacob *"took hold of Esau's heel,"* explaining how he contended or fought against his brother already from his mother's womb.[8]

Let's read Genesis 25:30-34:

> And Esau said to Jacob, "Please feed me with that same red stew, for I am weary." Therefore his name was called Edom. But Jacob said, "Sell me your birthright as of this day." And

Esau said, "Look, I am about to die; so what is this birthright to me?" Then Jacob said, "Swear to me as of this day." ...Thus Esau despised his birthright.

Esau was going through a difficult moment. He had just gotten back from hunting; he was exhausted and dying of hunger. His life was in danger. That is when he saw his brother Jacob, who had stayed in the camp and was preparing a soup.

The birthright was very important because it gave right to the father's inheritance, according to God's will, on the basis of which the birthright was consecrated to the Lord.

Jacob took advantage of Esau's desperation making his the blessing destined to the firstborn. Esau did not understand the value of this blessing; consequently, he was willing to give it away in a moment of need.

We too are *heirs* of the blessing according to the Scriptures. In fact, it is this blessing that establishes the difference between us and those who do not know God.

God has already put His total blessing on your life, even if you cannot understand it completely because of your scarce knowledge of the biblical promises that have to do with you. Not knowing the full value of this blessing, you could underestimate it like Esau did and run the risk of straying from the plan God has established for your life. Your circumstances and difficulties can become so critical to the point of hindering you from seeing beyond them. By losing sight of God, you will end up going astray from the way God has reserved for you.

Esau was in such distress that he declared, "Look, I am about to die," completely forgetting about being under God's blessing, to which he gave no importance at all. He was not able to recognize God's blessing over his life, and that the Lord would have never let him die but would have provided for him.

The enemy's work consists exactly in creating difficulties to make you go astray from the Lord's blessings. His strategy is to lie and use your circumstances to suggest that your life is not at all blessed.

In order to recognize and neutralize the effect of his lies, we have to be able to understand the enemy's stratagems. In fact, he works incessantly to hinder us from experiencing the blessings that are ours in Christ Jesus.

The third episode that concerns Jacob is in Genesis 27:26-27:

> *Then his father Isaac said to him, "Come near now and kiss me, my son." And he came near and kissed him; and he smelled the smell of his clothing, and blessed him and said: "Surely, the smell of my son is like the smell of a field which the Lord has blessed."*

Isaac, who was Jacob and Esau's father, was on the point of death. Before dying, tradition had it that a father would give his blessing to his children and in particular to the oldest. Jacob's mother, seeing that the time had come, told her son, "Jacob, put your brother's clothes on and go to your father who no longer sees well. Take Esau's place so you can receive his blessing."

What was the reason for this deception? The mother preferred Jacob, while the father was more affectionate toward Esau.

When examining these verses carefully, we see that, "Isaac blessed him and *said*." So blessings come through words, just as curses come through words.

You have to understand a fundamental truth—we are the fruit of what has been said about us and of the words in which we believed in the past.

Often parents are those who pronounce words of curse on their children's lives who then end up being the incarnation of evil words sown in precedence.

Blessings and curses can change people's lives. We pronounce them with our mouths and they can change the course of our existence.

So what are blessings? They are words of "good" spoken over people,[9] while curses are nothing else than words of "evil."[10]

For example, I bless someone when I say, "May you grow, may your family be happy, may your children be healthy and fully satisfied. May you have prosperity, joy, and peace!" But I can curse a child saying, "Everything you do is wrong! Look at your brother, he does everything right!" Through these words a child ends up forming a wrong self-image, believing in these phrases and acting consequently. People end up with low self-esteem and considering themselves as losers because somebody pronounced curses in the past!

We have to watch our tongues because the words that come out of our mouths always produce effects.[11]

Learn How to Bless

Therefore may God give you of the dew of heaven, of the fatness of the earth, and plenty of grain and wine. Let peoples serve you, and nations bow down to you. Be master over your brethren, and let your mother's sons bow down to you. Cursed be everyone who curses you, and blessed be those who bless you! (Genesis 27:28-29)

These are the blessing words that Isaac spoke over Jacob's life, convinced that he was his favorite firstborn, Esau.

Isaac had asked Esau to go hunting and cook for him so that he could eat a delicious meal.[12] While Esau was still out hunting, Isaac was deceived on his deathbed by his wife Rebekah and his son Jacob. As soon as the blessing was given, Esau came back from hunting and this is what happened, "But he said, 'Your brother came with deceit and has taken away your blessing'" (Gen. 27:35).

So Jacob *obtained* the blessing through deception! And the blessing was on him!

In Genesis 27:36-40 we can read Esau's reaction:

And Esau said, "Is he not rightly named Jacob?[13] For he has supplanted me these two times. He took away my birthright, and now look, he has taken away my blessing!" And he said, "Have you not reserved a blessing for me?" Then Isaac answered and said to Esau, "Indeed I have made him your master, and all his brethren I have given to him as servants; with grain and wine I have sustained him. What shall I do now for you, my son?" And Esau said to his father, "Have you only one blessing, my father? Bless me also, O my father!" And Esau lifted up his voice and wept. Then Isaac his father answered and said to him: "Behold, your dwelling shall be of the fatness of the earth, and of the dew of heaven from above. By your sword you shall live, and you shall serve your brother; and it shall come to pass, when you become restless, that you shall break his yoke from your neck."[14]

GOD'S BLESSINGS ARE PRECIOUS

Here is another episode of Jacob's life that helps us fully understand the importance and the value of God's blessing in our lives.

Then Jacob was left alone; and a Man wrestled with him until the breaking of day. Now when He saw that He did not prevail against him, He touched the socket of his hip; and the socket of Jacob's hip was out of joint as He wrestled with him. And He said, "Let Me go, for the day breaks." But he said, "I will not let You go unless You bless me!" So He said to him, "What is your name?" He said, "Jacob." And He said, "Your name shall no longer be called Jacob, but Israel; for you have struggled with God and with men, and have prevailed." Then Jacob asked, saying, "Tell me Your name, I pray." And He said, "Why is it that you ask about My name?" And He blessed him there (Genesis 32:24-29).

These verses immediately highlight that Jacob was a fighter. Sure, he was a cheater, but he also was a man who knew how to do something good: fight. He did it with an aim: to obtain the blessing!

In those days people trusted in God's blessings. In the Old Testament we continuously see how God's blessings changed people's lives. What are we to do to receive God's blessings today? In the Old Testament Jacob teaches us to fight in order to obtain them, but how should we act today that we live in the New Testament era? Under grace we no longer have to fight, but simply *believe* in the blessings![15] In the Old Testament it was necessary to fight physically to obtain them; today all we have to do is believe to make them ours. In fact, we are fighting a battle of faith.

Before leaving with my family for Bible school, I received this Word from God, "If you obey, you will eat the best products of the country." Once I completed my studies, after several useless work experiences and many years after that word, I was sent to preach in a Sicilian town. I accepted with great joy.

One day when I finished preaching, a man came up to me asking for my car keys. While handing them to him, I thought that perhaps for some reason he needed to move the car. When time came to leave, I found my car overwhelmed with boxes of fruit, vegetables, oil, and lots of other goods. I was thankful for that abundance and I noticed that on the boxes there was written: "The best products of the Country." In that moment I remembered the promise God had made me years before. I thanked the Lord for His faithfulness while abundant tears ran down my face.

Our Father God's generosity, mindfulness, and faithfulness toward His children are wonderful! All we have to do in order to receive from His hands is believe in Him and in His promises.[16]

Christ Is Your Blessing Today

The Old Testament presents God's blessing in terms of prosperity through the images of oil or wine. The land was blessed so that it could produce abundant fruit.

Therefore, the blessing is very important for our lives, and Jacob's continuous pursuit and willingness to do anything to obtain it reminds us of this truth.

The New Testament talks about the blessing as well: "Blessed be the God and Father of our Lord Jesus Christ, who has blessed us with every spiritual blessing in the heavenly places in Christ" (Ephesians 1:3).

If in the Old Testament Jacob pursued the blessings, even more so do we need to believe that we *have already been* blessed with *every* spiritual blessing in the heavenly places in Christ Jesus!

This means that when you choose to believe in Christ, you are blessed with every type of spiritual blessing. The Bible says that if we are in Christ, then God the Father has blessed us in an overabundant way with every type of spiritual blessing. Such blessings have been declared on the lives of each one of us!

In the light of what we have said, if we keep on telling ourselves and others that we are not very lucky people, all we are doing is considering God a liar, although we know that God never lies.[17]

The moment we accept Jesus as our personal Savior and become Christians, each one of us is blessed. These blessings have to do with our future just as much as with our present, that is our daily lives, and they translate into actual *things*: a new job, healing, a new house, a trip.

If we are having a hard time making it to the end of the month with our salary, that does not mean that we are not living under the blessing, but rather that we have to renew our minds.[18]

What is the renewal of the mind? It means that you have to change your self-image, knowing deep inside your heart that you are blessed because Christ is in you! By doing so, you will inherit or experience the blessings that are already yours. However, this awareness comes by knowing the Word of God. This is why I keep insisting on the need to study and meditate on His Word.

Get rid of the thoughts that the enemy is suggesting to you, trying to convince you with these words, "You won't make it! What do you think you're doing? You can't make it! You'll never have the money you need to do what you want." It is a continuous battle through which he tries to make you believe in failure. We have to make a choice: either believe in the words of the enemy or in the

Word of God! Personally, I have decided to refuse all thoughts of defeat and firmly believe in what the Bible says.[19]

Eat at the Table Laid out for You

It is necessary to read, study, and memorize the Scriptures, but this is not sufficient. In fact, these three activities represent only the preparation for a more complete meditation.

It is true that the Lord has blessed us, but if we do not set our eyes on God we will not make any blessings ours because we ignore having already been blessed with every blessing.[20]

As a pastor, I can explain what your position is in Jesus Christ and I can serve you this food without great effort. However, this will not be of great benefit until you have the personal revelation that you are sitting in the heavenly places at the right hand of the Father through Christ Jesus!

Faith is a personal responsibility.[21] As pastors, we can prepare a *tasty meal*, but it is not sufficient to look at it from a distance. You have to come up to the table and get what is yours by rights, and eat until you are satisfied. Eat what your pastor has prepared for you. Read the Scriptures mentioned and meditate on them. Taste this savoring food and smell the scent coming from the table; eat and assimilate because this is the only way you can bring fruit into your life![22]

The Word of God can produce fruit in your life only if you eat it. It is not sufficient to go to church on Sundays or simply listen to someone explain the Scriptures under the anointing. This will not change your life because there is a lack of personal meditation of the Scriptures. If you mirror yourself every day in the Word of God, as you mirror yourself before leaving the house, then your life will change and you will know the right direction you are to follow in every circumstance of your life.[23]

Be a Person after God's Heart

Nobody has innate knowledge. We all have to learn how to take on personal responsibility and feed ourselves with the food of the

Word. Everybody can receive *"every* spiritual blessing in the heavenly places in Christ."[24] Since we are in Christ Jesus, we have already been blessed! But we will make these blessings ours in the measure according to which we receive the revelation of the Scriptures.

Proverbs 26:2 says that, "A curse without cause shall not alight." What does this mean? What triggers curses in our lives? The main cause is a lifestyle based on sin, which is being far from God and never setting your eyes on Him.

Setting our eyes on God does not mean praying day and night. In fact, you can be far from God even if you pray. It rather has to do with being close to God's heart, loving Him, getting to know Him and worshiping Him.

In order to better understand this concept, here is a verse from Hebrews 12:16-17:

> *Lest there be any fornicator or profane person like Esau, who for one morsel of food sold his birthright. For you know that afterward, when he wanted to inherit the blessing, he was rejected, for he found no place for repentance, though he sought it diligently with tears.*

The Bible says that tears are not always a sign of repentance. Many people cry without showing any trace of repentance. Without sincere repentance, tears do not mean much. They indicate only a desire to follow rules, but deep inside the heart it is not so. Why is sincere repentance so important in a Christian's life?[25] Repentance basically consists in recognizing that you have made a mistake and in manifesting your will to change direction.

Repentance produces a change in your way of reasoning, which consequently causes a change in your actions.

With Repentance Comes Healing and Comfort

When we do what is wrong in God's eyes, tears are not enough. In fact, crying does not have the ability to generate any change of direction, but only a probable reiteration of the sin. A wrong action, not corrected by repentance, leaves the door open for the enemy who enters undisturbed bringing curses into your life. Instead, when you go to God with sincere repentance recognizing your wrongdoings, the blood of Jesus cleanses you from your sins and you receive the ability to change direction by modifying your lifestyle. You will stumble and fall again, but you will have the strength to stand back up because you decided to turn your back on sin.[26]

Esau cried but he did not receive any blessing because his tears did not express repentance. Where there is repentance, there is always healing and comfort.

God answers to sincere repentance, as we can see in Hosea 14:1-3. In this circumstance the wrongdoing had to do with the whole people:

> O Israel, return to the Lord your God, for you have stumbled because of your iniquity; take words with you, and return to the Lord. Say to Him, "Take away all iniquity; receive us graciously, for we will offer the sacrifices of our lips. Assyria shall not save us, we will not ride on horses, nor will we say anymore to the work of our hands, 'You are our gods.' For in You the fatherless finds mercy."

A seriously repented person says: "I will trust in no one else but You. I will no longer trust in my own strength. I know I have done wrong against You. I have been proud. I thought I could make it on my own, but I was wrong. Lord, I repent!"

God will move in answer to sincere repentance:

> I will heal their backsliding, I will love them freely, for My anger has turned away from him. I will be like the dew to Israel; he shall grow like the lily, and lengthen his roots like Lebanon. His branches shall spread; his beauty shall be like an olive tree, and his fragrance like Lebanon. Those who dwell under his shadow shall return; they shall be revived like grain, and grow like a vine. Their scent shall be like the wine of Lebanon (Hosea 14:4-7).

When we repent, God says, "I will restore you. You will be like a grain of wheat, you will bloom like a flower, you will be renowned!"[27]

Through sincere repentance, God brings us back to the state of grace as children. We have already been blessed, but we have to walk in God's blessing.

CHRIST JESUS HAS BLESSED YOUR LIFE

We have been blessed in the heavenly places in Christ Jesus and therefore God's blessing *is already* on our lives.

Let's read Galatians 3:8-9, "And the Scripture, foreseeing that God would justify the Gentiles by faith, preached the Gospel to Abraham beforehand, saying, 'In you all the nations shall be blessed.' So then those who are of faith are blessed with believing Abraham."

In the Old Testament, the blessing was a promise. In the New Testament, the promise was fulfilled in Christ Jesus.

In the Old Testament, the blessing was a promise of which one had to take possession by fighting. In the New Testament, all promises have been fulfilled and our battle consists in *believing* and *acting in faith*.

We have to fight the battle that consists in believing that we have already been blessed and that God will take care of all our needs. It is no longer a physical battle, but a battle of faith.

Let's carefully read Acts 3:25-26, "You are sons of the prophets, and of the covenant which God made with our fathers, saying to Abraham, 'And in your seed all the families of the earth shall be blessed. To you first, God, having raised up His Servant Jesus, sent Him to bless you, in turning away every one of you from your iniquities.'"

The Scriptures say that Jesus was sent with a purpose: *"To bless you."*

Jesus was *specially* sent so that we could receive the blessing. In Abraham we become heirs of the blessing, not of the curse!

Sickness and poverty are a curse, but the Scriptures teach us that healing and prosperity are a blessing. The lives of the fathers of faith were full of prosperity. All the fathers of faith were wealthy and not poor—Abraham was rich, Isaac was rich, Jacob was rich, Joseph was rich, David was rich.

"But Jesus was poor! He was born in a stable. He lay in a manger!" you might object. But the Bible says that Jesus gave up His riches in heaven, not that he was poor. He became poor because he left His heavenly riches behind Him.[28] When comparing His earthly riches with His heavenly ones, he certainly was poor, but at the same time His life and His ministry were supported by several women, among whom was Joanna, the wife of Chuza, Herod's steward.[29] This shows us that Jesus was not a beggar. Although He was born in a manger, He immediately received gold, incense, and myrrh, gifts usually destined for kings.

Jesus Freely Gives and Perfects Faith

There are moments in which we are obliged to live in the cave. We feel discouraged, full of fear and lacking in any support. However, we have a certainty that we can come out of that place and reach our final destiny setting our eyes on Jesus.

Our victory begins when we have the kind of faith that says, "I am blessed! I am ill, but the Bible says that with the stripes of Jesus Christ I am healed.[30] In the name of Jesus on whom I keep my eyes set, I prophesize blessing over my life."

What does it mean *to call or prophesize blessing over your life?*

Let's see what the Scriptures say. Isaac declared blessings over Jacob and Esau: "By faith Isaac blessed Jacob and Esau concerning things to come" (Heb. 11:20).

Isaac declared blessings through words. He believed in what he said. He blessed them concerning things to come! Each one of us can bless our lives with our *words*.

If we firmly believe that we have been blessed with every spiritual blessing in the heavenly places in Christ, as Ephesians 1:3 says, then we will walk with our eyes set on Jesus, acting according to what pleases God and not going astray.

Consequently, the blessing will be on us and we will walk in it. We inherit the blessings *prophesying* or *declaring* ourselves blessed concerning things to come.

You cannot change your past, but you can mold your present and your future. The past is past. What happened has happened, but those who believe in Christ Jesus and are in Him have the ability to give form to their present and future.

We can improve or transform our present and future thanks to the words that come out of our mouths. Through our words we can change our lives, those of our families, of the people around us, our neighborhood and our city, our nation and the world.

Many things can come into being or be changed through words of faith!

Two Kinds of Faith: Thomas's and Christ's

God is the author and the model of our faith. In the first chapter of Genesis we see how God created all visible things through His Word, which is *speaking*, "God said...and things were."

Faith "*calleth* those things which be not as though they were" (Rom. 4:17 KJV).

If you are ill, declare healing over your life. If you are poor, declare financial prosperity. Declare blessings over you and your loved ones, because faith calls things which are not as though they were.

I am not suggesting to call into being things that do not exist, but rather to call things that already exist and *are not yet visible*. Where are the things that *already exist*? In the Bible. If I desire prosperity or blessing, the Word is the answer.

We can see changes in our lives by declaring healing even if we are not healed yet, prosperity even if at present we have nothing, a new job when we are unemployed and so on for every kind of blessing, because the Bible says that we have already been blessed!

Faith enables us to believe even before seeing.

Jesus said to Thomas, "Thomas, because you have seen Me, you have believed. Blessed are those who have not seen and yet have believed" (John 20:29).

Thomas's faith was the kind that had *to touch in order to believe*. However, we have to distinguish between the two kinds of faith. The first is Thomas's, who believes only in evidence that is in front of him. The second is that of those who, not seeing, believe that Jesus has already paid for them and therefore obtain what they cannot touch. These are the two kinds of faith in which we move every day.

The first kind of faith, which operates in touching and seeing, is the material kind of faith, which is of our natural senses. Christian faith believes in the supernatural, in what goes beyond the physical world for which we use our senses. This is the *faith of God*, which goes *beyond* the natural.[31] It enables us to believe even before seeing, and therefore calls those things which still are not as if they were. This faith makes the invisible things visible and translates God's promises into actual things.

We have already been blessed! We have to believe in this truth with all our hearts and confess with our mouths that we are blessed in Christ Jesus. Then we will really receive every blessing.

This is what David and the 400 men did. They decided to come out of the cave and to follow God, mirroring themselves in His Word and firmly believing in His promises.

Chapter Eight

COME OUT
OF THE CAVE

THE LORD IS YOUR REFUGE

He who dwells in the secret place of the Most High shall abide under the shadow of the Almighty. I will say of the Lord, "He is my refuge and my fortress; my God, in Him I will trust." Surely He shall deliver you from the snare of the fowler and from the perilous pestilence. He shall cover you with His feathers, and under His wings you shall take refuge; His truth shall be your shield and buckler" (Psalm 91:1-4).

David took refuge in the cave where he learned how to go down to the rock, which represents Christ. Here he learned and taught how to cry out to the Lord and trust in Him. God answered in a compassionate and powerful way, helping David and his men to come out of that place more than conquerors.

God has not changed. He still looks at His children through the eyes and the heart of a loving Father. By reading His Word, we know that He has already prepared everything for our well-being, establishing our roles and how to inherit His promises in this life, through the progressive and voluntary renewal of our minds.

In this last chapter, we will see how God not only has freely given us everything through His Son's sacrifice, but how He has also surrounded us with a supernatural protection that enables us to have access to the heavenly resources in every moment of our lives.

Go to Your Father—You Are His Child!

When we talk about *refuge in God*, we know that it is a place where we can find total and complete protection. When we cry out to God, He answers saying, *"Sure,* I'll deliver you." All we have to say is, "Lord, You are my refuge!"

> *Because you have made the Lord, who is my refuge, even the Most High, your dwelling place, no evil shall befall you, nor shall any plague come near your dwelling* (Psalm 91:9-10).

We have to make these words our own. When we wake up in the morning, before going to sleep at night, in every moment of joy or sorrow, we should declare with all our hearts, "Lord, You are my refuge!" The Word assures us that when we make the Almighty our refuge, nothing will harm us. This is one of the many promises that God has made us.[1] Therefore, fully believe that the Lord is your refuge!

Do we not all need some kind of deliverance in our lives? So let's cry out to the Lord, "You are my refuge!"

It is not sufficient to think or say those words, but rather we need to declare them. Faith comes from hearing the Word of God.[2] When we go to the Lord, something happens at a spiritual level—we invite God *to be present* in our circumstances, just like a child would do with his or her father.

With extreme naturalness and spontaneity, every child, when in difficulty, asks for help and protection from his or her parent. In the same way, believers have to ask protection from He who has made us His children through the greatest sacrifice in history.[3]

This is what David taught his men, giving the example. He entered the cave as a shepherd and came out as a king. Wouldn't you like to be a king, too?

Do you know that the Bible says that in Christ Jesus we are a people of kings and queens?[4] We are called to reign in this life with Jesus. Therefore, believing that we are kings is in no way whatsoever a form of pride, but simply a declaration of what the Word says about us.

When we learn how to see ourselves through God's eyes, we stop seeing only our mistakes and failures, and start considering ourselves through God's eyes, knowing that we have a Father who takes care of us and *supports us*. It is as if God is on the terraces holding flags and trumpets while shouting, "Come on! You can make it. You will make it! I'm with you! I'm sending My angels to help you." This is what He does.

People often talk about angels. But what are they really? Fat puttos with little wings flying here and there according to the classic iconography?

Let's read what the Bible says about angels, "For He shall give His angels charge over you, to keep you in all your ways" (Ps. 91:11).

Have you ever heard anyone talk about guardian angels? Before becoming a believer, I was convinced that angels were part of a fairy tale to help children fall asleep. Today I know that this is not so because the Bible testifies of their existence. Angels are real.

The Scriptures tell us that we are surrounded by angles and that they take care of us. We are often not capable of recognizing their presence due to our ignorance.[5]

Jesus said to those who had believed in Him, "If you abide in My word, you are My disciples indeed. And you shall know the truth, and the truth shall make you free" (John 8:31-32). The great obstacle in our lives is the fact of ignoring the truth. This is why I would like to conclude by explicitly talking about angels.

Cry Out to God, He Will Send Help

Let's read Psalm 91:11 again, "For He shall give His angels charge over you, to keep you in all your ways." This verse declares that God sends His angels to protect you.

When you start believing in God, you will be able to discern the presence or the action of these creatures. Let's study them together and discover their dynamics. You might have felt evil presences around you before. Such presences are nothing else than rebellious angels. However, you might have felt kind, embracing, and protective presences around you transmitting love and peace. These presences are God's angels, a biblical reality.

When you cry out to the Lord, something happens in the spiritual world. Angels start moving because, as the Scriptures say, the Lord "shall give His angels charge over you, to keep you in *all* your ways."

It is not written in some of your ways, but in *all* your ways! In Psalm 91 verses 12 and 13 we read their God-given assignment, "In their hands they shall bear you up, lest you dash your foot against a stone. You shall tread upon the lion and the cobra, the young lion and the serpent you shall trample underfoot."

Another verse in the Scriptures says that their role is to continuously look over our children, "Take heed that you do not despise one of these little ones, for I say to you that in heaven their angels always see the face of My Father who is in heaven" (Matt. 18:10).

Do not despise children, do not commit any violence against them. Respect them, take care of their lives. Each one of them has an angel at their side living *continuously* at the presence of the Father!

Take Refuge under the Father's Wings

Let's observe some examples of what angels do in obedience to God's will.

Lot was led out of Sodom and Gomorrah, cities of vice, thanks to the guidance of an angel.[6] On two different occasions, Peter was set free from prison thanks to an angel who opened the cell doors and those of the actual prison.[7]

To better understand the reality of angels, let's observe what happened to Elisha. The king of Syria attacked Israel, but despite his efforts he could not manage to overcome. In fact, Elisha would reveal to the king of Israel the enemy's strategies before they could attack. The king of Syria was informed that Israel's success was due to the prophet who knew by revelation what was decided in secret. So he sent his army to seize the man of God.

> *Then the king of Israel sent someone to the place of which the man of God had told him. Thus he warned him, and he was watchful there, not just once or twice. Therefore the heart of the king of Syria was greatly troubled by this thing; and he called his servants and said to them, "Will you not show me which of us is for the king of Israel?" And one of his servants said, "None, my lord, O king; but Elisha, the prophet who is in Israel, tells the king of Israel the words that you speak in your bedroom." So he said, "Go and see where he is, that I may send and get him." And it was told him, saying, "Surely he is in Dothan." Therefore he sent horses and chariots and a great army there, and they came by night and surrounded the city* (2 Kings 6:10-14).

The king sent a great army with horses and chariots to arrest one single man! Imagine seeing at the horizon an army advancing toward you. An army of enemies attacking your life. A great amount of debts, illnesses, or difficulties. What would you do if you knew that you could not make resistance because they outnumbered you? Would you be overcome by despair, or would you decide to take refuge in God? If you take refuge in God, do you have the certainty that things will change?

THE TRUE SOURCE OF LIFE

The previous paragraph finishes with an unanswered question. The following is an exhaustive answer to that question through the Word of God.

Let's read Second Kings 6:15-16:

> *And when the servant of the man of God arose early and went out, there was an army, surrounding the city with horses and chariots. And his servant said to him, "Alas, my master! What shall we do?" So he answered, "Do not fear, for those who are with us are more than those who are with them."*

Imagine the scene. You wake up in the morning, open the window, and discover that you are surrounded by an entire army of soldiers with horses and chariots. You have no means of escape. But the man of God says, *"Do not fear."*

Fear is the opposite of faith. When we let ourselves be overridden by fear, we are no longer capable of acting. We end up undergoing the enemy's attack without being capable of fighting back. Fear leaves us uncovered; we are no longer protected by our shield. The Bible says that our shield is faith.[8] So fear deprives us of the shield of faith that God gave us to protect us!

Ask for Full Revelation of the Word

The prophet's first words were, *"Do not fear,"* and then he added, "For those who are with us are more than those who are with them." After such a statement, the servant could have asked Elisha what he had drunk for breakfast, because there was an army camped in front of them! All they had to do was make one step and they would have been destroyed. How could that poor servant remain calm when seeing that they were surrounded by an army? So the man of God prayed, "Lord, I pray, open his eyes that he may see" (2 Kings 6:17).

The servant saw the enemy with his natural eyes, but those of his heart were closed. The verse continues saying, "Then the Lord opened the eyes of the young man, and he saw. And behold, the mountain was full of horses and chariots of fire all around Elisha."

The servant received a new visual capacity that enabled him to see the invisible, although real, hosts of God. With his eyes open on the spiritual world, he could see the enemy already defeated, because God had put His angels on the battlefield to protect His servant.

Sometimes we ask God to intervene in our lives without "seeing" what He has already provided. The most appropriate way to pray in such case is the following, "Lord, open the eyes of my heart so that I can fully believe in what is written and can receive a complete revelation of Your Word." The revelation of the Word changes our circumstances! Knowing the whole Bible by heart or studying it in depth does not produce great changes inside and around us! What changes our hearts toward our circumstances is keeping the Word in us and meditating on it. In fact, true transformation takes place only in the heart. It is in the heart that true changes take place, manifesting themselves in our lives.

Please continue reading this passage from the Scriptures in your personal time and discover how God intervened to save Elisha and his servant.

Angels Serve the Heirs of Salvation

To further analyze the dynamics and the roles of angels, I would like to share another Scripture:

> *Are they not all ministering spirits sent forth to minister for those who will inherit salvation?* (Hebrews 1:14)

These words reveal that angels are sent forth to serve those who inherit salvation, that is believers! The Word, as you can see, is the source of revelation; it generates faith that moves mountains.[9] It is vitally important to preach the Gospel because it is the power of God for whoever believes.[10] So if you do not first believe with all your heart, God's power cannot manifest itself in your life.

Some time ago I was in Verona, Italy, for the inauguration of the academic year of the Rhema Bible School.[11] A pastor from the Bible school in Bristol, England, had been invited to speak.

The man talked about a period in his life in which he did not have the money to even buy bread for his family. Not knowing what to do, he started looking for a job, even just washing dishes, to earn the necessary money to support his family and carry on with his evening studies. In the meantime, he continued trusting in God.

One day looking out of his house window he saw a tree full of apples in his neighbor's garden. Moved by hunger, he and his family expressed the desire to eat at least one of those fruits. Shortly after, they heard someone knock at the door: It was an elderly lady offering them a basket full of those wonderful apples.

They were so surprised and happy for the unexpected gift that they forgot to thank the woman. So the man ran out immediately to thank and bless her for that act of generosity. He knocked at the neighbor's door only to find out that the house was vacant and had been empty for a long time. In that moment the pastor recognized the hand of God. That lady had to be an angel sent by the Father to provide for his family's needs.

We often think that we should trouble God only for serious situations, when in reality He wants to take care of us always and in every circumstance.

God is interested in our everyday lives! He is the Father who takes care of us. He knows us by name and even knows the number of hairs on our heads.[12]

Celebrate with the Angels

I could give you many more testimonies, but I will finish simply reminding you of several things.

First I would like to ask you a question, "Do you know that the angels in heaven celebrate when a sinner repents on the earth?"[13]

Every time someone on the earth accepts Jesus into his or her life, there is joy in heaven. So if angels celebrate in heaven, why do most churches on earth not manifest such joy and are quite the opposite, gloomy and sad?

If God's presence abides in church, why do we have to remain composed and silent? If there is great joy in heaven, then let's celebrate here as well!

We have to learn how to be joyful, to celebrate and rejoice in God's presence.

The Bible says that in His presence there is abundance of joy and never-ending pleasures.[14]

We should rejoice for the presence of angels in our lives. The Bible says that angels obey God's will. "Bless the Lord, you His angels, who excel in strength, who do His word, heeding the voice of His word" (Ps. 103:20).

So angels are *powerful and strong*, and not small and plump as they are often represented. They draw their joy from the Word of the Lord. There are myriads of angels divided in ranks: cherubs, seraphs, archangels, and so on.

Although angels are powerful and strong executors of God's will, the Bible teaches us not to worship them.

"Let no one cheat you of your reward, taking delight in false humility and worship of angels" (Col. 2:18). Angels are not God, and actually we are superior to them because we are made in the image and likeness of God.[15]

People around us carry the image and likeness of God regardless if they are believers or not, because we all have been created in His image. So we all are *wonderful*, for God creates only masterpieces.

Your beauty is not recognized by everybody and perhaps you do not see beauty in yourself, but God does. When He looks at you, He is pleased with you as a father looking at his children.

I love God because He does not judge me and does not condemn me. He understands me and leads me toward change.

Worship God and Him Alone

The apostle John said in Revelation 22:8-9, "I fell down to worship before the feet of the angel who showed me these things."

The angel answered, saying, "See that you do not do that. For I am your fellow servant, and of your brethren the prophets, and of those who keep the words of this book. Worship God!"

From this verse we learn something else about angels—they are "fellow servants" of those who keep the words of this Book.

Angels are pure spirit, whose presence cannot be recognized without the gift of "discerning of spirits."[16]

The Bible says that angels are spirits sent to serve those who inherit eternal life. Therefore, angels are our servants. God takes care of us through these creatures even when we are not aware of them.

Honor Yourself and You Will Honor God

I would like to finish this journey with a Scripture from the book of Hebrews.

Do not forget the angel's words when John bowed down in front of its beauty. The angel made him stand up and said, "Don't worship me!" And then added: "Worship God!" Are these not the words of the first commandment? "You shall worship the Lord your God, and Him only you shall serve" (Matt. 4:10).

Do you think that worship takes place in church? Do you know what the Bible says in this regard?

The first worship to God has to do with how you treat yourself.[17] If as soon as you get up in the morning you say, "I'm in a bad situation! I'm nothing! I'm worth nothing! I can't make it anymore!" you are not giving God honor and worship.

Until you recognize the presence of God in you, you cannot define yourself a real believer. Learn how to recognize the presence of Christ in you, and He who is in you will manifest Himself also around you.

It is important to pay attention to this simple teaching so that God's presence may manifest itself through us!

The first way Jesus manifests Himself through us is the same way we allowed Him to come into our lives: "For with the heart one believes...and with the mouth confession is made...."[18]

The best way to manifest God's presence in you is by using your mouth. How? You need to say, "Lord, You are my refuge!" and the Lord will send forth His angels. You speak and believe and therefore act according to the Word while God answers. Your confession of faith enables Him to move in a supernatural way. Even if you cannot see things happening in the invisible kingdom, angels are at work serving those who have inherited salvation.

> *Let brotherly love continue. Do not forget to entertain strangers, for by so doing some have unwittingly entertained angels* (Hebrews 13:1-2).

Let's keep on loving those around us and not deprive ourselves of this joy. Let's not forget hospitality by sharing what we have with those who have less or come from another nation. They could be angels sent from God to bless us.

Let's expand our boundaries as Jesus invites us to do. He expanded them to the point of giving Himself with the love He has for us. Now He is sitting at the right of the Father and is interceding for us, moved by the same unchangeable and unconditional love. He loved us first and completed His work to the end.

Now it is up to us to do our part!

ENDNOTES

CHAPTER TWO

1. Acts 13:22, "And when He had removed him [Saul, the first king of Israel], He raised up for them David as king, to whom also He gave testimony [God Himself gave testimony to David!] and said, 'I have found David the son of Jesse, a man after My own heart, who will do all My will.'"

2. Genesis 41:38-40, "And Pharaoh said to his servants, 'Can we find such a one as this, a man in whom is the Spirit of God?' Then Pharaoh said to Joseph, 'Inasmuch as God has shown you all this, there is no one as discerning and wise as you. You shall be over my house, and all my people shall be ruled according to your word; only in regard to the throne will I be greater than you.'"

3. James 1:5-6, "If any of you lacks wisdom, let him ask of God, who gives to all liberally and without reproach, and it will be given to him. But let him ask in faith, with no doubting, for he who doubts is like a wave of the sea driven and tossed by the wind."

4. See 1 Corinthians 12:7-11.

5. 1 Corinthians 11:1, "Imitate me, just as I also imitate Christ." Paul said to the Corinthians: "Follow my example, because I follow the best example ever—the Word and Christ's works."

6. Philippians 4:19, "And my God shall supply all your need according to His riches in glory by Christ Jesus."

7. Proverbs 3:9-10, "Honor the Lord with your possessions, and with the firstfruits of all your increase; so your barns will be filled with plenty, and your vats will overflow with new wine."

8. 1 Chronicles 11:10, "Now these were the heads of the mighty men whom David had, who strengthened themselves with him in his kingdom, with all Israel, to make him king, according to the word of the Lord concerning Israel."

9. See Nehemiah 8:10.

10. 1 John 2:27, "But the anointing which you have received from Him [from God through Christ] abides in you, and you do not need that anyone teach you; but as the same anointing teaches you concerning all things, and is true, and is not a lie, and just as it has taught you, you will abide in Him." The word "anointing" indicates that the Holy Spirit is in us. It is the presence of Christ in us to guide us, love us, bless us, and to call us to serve God in all His ways. Through the anointing we are supernaturally equipped to accomplish the works to which every Christian is called.

11. Hebrews 6:12, "...imitate those who through faith and patience inherit the promises."

12. 2 Corinthians 1:20, "For all the promises of God in Him are Yes, and in Him Amen...." They are "yes" because He has already made them, and "amen" because He is faithful to fulfill them.

13. Malachi 3:10, "'Bring all the tithes into the storehouse, that there may be food in My house, and try Me now in this,' says the Lord of hosts, 'If I will not open for you the windows of heaven and pour out for you such blessing that there will not be room enough to receive it.'"

14. Luke 4:43, "...I [Jesus] must preach the kingdom of God to the other cities also, because for this purpose I have been sent."

15. 1 Samuel 16:7, "...For the Lord does not see as man sees; for man looks at the outward appearance, but the Lord looks at the heart."

16. 1 Corinthians 10:4, "And all [our fathers] drank the same spiritual drink. For they drank of that spiritual Rock that followed them, and that Rock was Christ."

17. 1 Peter 5:8, "Be sober, be vigilant; because your adversary the devil walks about like a roaring lion, seeking whom he may devour."

CHAPTER THREE

1. Jesus, the Lamb of God who takes away the sins of the world, was offered once and for all! His blood washed away all sins and through His sacrifice we have inherited all of God's promises.

2. Ephesians 2:8-10, "For by grace you have been saved through faith, and that not of yourselves; it is the gift of God, not of works, lest anyone should boast. For we are His workmanship, created in Christ Jesus for good works, which God prepared beforehand that we should walk in them." Everything we have belongs to God, it is the fruit of a gift from God that has been given to us by grace.

3. Romans 4:20-25, "He [Abraham] did not waver at the promise of God through unbelief, but was strengthened in

faith, giving glory to God, and being fully convinced that what He had promised He was also able to perform. And therefore 'it was accounted to him for righteousness.' Now it was not written for his sake alone that it was imputed to him, but also for us. It shall be imputed to us who believe in Him who raised up Jesus our Lord from the dead...."

4. Genesis 18:19, "For I [God] have known him, in order that he may command his children and his household after him, that they keep the way of the Lord, to do righteousness and justice, that the Lord may bring to Abraham what He has spoken to him."

5. Remember what is written: "...a doer of the work will be blessed in what he does." Read James 1:22-25.

6. 2 Corinthians 9:6-7, "...He who sows sparingly will also reap sparingly, and he who sows bountifully will also reap bountifully. So let each one give as he purposes in his heart, not grudgingly or of necessity; for God loves a cheerful giver."

7. *To reveal* literally means "to unveil, to say what is not known, not very clear or hidden." Jeremiah 33:3, "Call to Me, and I will answer you, and show you great and mighty things, which you do not know." Read also Daniel 2:22-23; Psalm 49:3; Psalm 119:99.

8. See http://www.capri.it/it/grotta-azzurra.

9. John 8:31-32, "Then Jesus said to those Jews who believed Him, 'If you abide in My word, you are My disciples indeed. And you shall know the truth, and the truth shall make you free.'"

10. Revelation 1:5-6, "...Jesus Christ, the faithful witness, the firstborn from the dead, and the ruler over the kings of the earth. And has made us kings and priests to His God and Father...." Read also Revelation 5:1-10.

11. Mark 2:3-4, "Then they came to Him, bringing a paralytic who was carried by four men. And when they could not come near Him because of the crowd, they uncovered the roof where He was. So when they had broken through, they let down the bed on which the paralytic was lying."

12. See Mark 10:46-52.

13. Isaiah 55:11, "So shall My word be that goes forth from My mouth; It shall not return to Me void, but it shall accomplish what I please, and it shall prosper in the thing for which I sent it."

14. Psalm 91:4, "He shall cover you with His feathers, and under His wings you shall take refuge; His truth shall be your shield and buckler."

15. See Hebrews 9:4.

16. See Matthew 27:50-54.

Chapter Four

1. The expression "corporative prayer" means a group of people gathered to pray together in agreement among each other so as to reach a common aim, having the same thoughts of victory and a heart sincerely open to believe in what the Word of God says. Read Acts 1:14; Acts 2:1.

2. Exodus 32:32-33, [Moses interceding for his people before God] "'Yet now, if You will forgive their sin but if not, I pray, blot me out of Your book which You have written' And the Lord said to Moses, 'Whoever has sinned against Me, I will blot him out of My book.'"

3. Revelation 21:27, "But there shall by no means enter it [in the heavenly Jerusalem] anything that defiles, or causes an abomination or a lie, but only those who are written in the Lamb's Book of Life."

4. 2 Samuel 22:2-3, "The Lord is my rock and my fortress and my deliverer; the God of my strength, in whom I will trust; my shield and the horn of my salvation, my stronghold and my refuge."

5. Matthew 17:20, [Jesus speaking to the apostles] "...I say to you, if you have faith as a mustard seed, you will say to this mountain, 'Move from here to there,' and it will move; and nothing will be impossible for you."

6. Galatians 4:4-7, "...God sent forth His Son, born of a woman, born under the law, to redeem those who were under the law, that we might receive the adoption as sons. And because you are sons, God has sent forth the Spirit of His Son into your hearts, crying out, 'Abba, Father!' Therefore you are no longer a slave but a son, and if a son, then an heir of God through Christ."

7. Isaiah 48:3, "I have declared the former things from the beginning; they went forth from my mouth, and I caused them to hear it. Suddenly I did them, and they came to pass."

8. Genesis 1:26, "Then God said, 'Let Us make man in Our image, according to Our likeness; let them have dominion over the fish of the sea, over the birds of the air, and over the cattle, over all the earth and over every creeping thing that creeps on the earth.'"

9. Numbers 22:28, "Then the Lord opened the mouth of the donkey, and she said to Balaam, 'What have I done to you, that you have struck me these three times?'"

10. Jeremiah 29:11-14, "'For I know the thoughts that I think toward you,' says the Lord, 'thoughts of peace and not of evil, to give you a future and a hope. Then you will call upon Me and go and pray to Me, and I will listen to you. And you will seek Me and find Me, when you search for Me with all your heart. I will be found by you....'"

11. When you accept Jesus Christ in your life, you make a personal confession of faith saying with your mouth that Jesus is your personal Savior, confession in which you believe with all your heart. Romans 10:9-10, "That if you confess with your mouth the Lord Jesus and believe in your heart that God has raised Him from the dead, you will be saved. For with the heart one believes unto righteousness, and with the mouth confession is made unto salvation."

12. Matthew 26:28, "For this is My blood of the new covenant, which is shed for many for the remission of sins." Revelation 7:13b, "Who are these arrayed in white robes, and where did they come from?"

13. 2 Corinthians 5:17, "Therefore, if anyone is in Christ, he is a new creation; old things have passed away; behold, all things have become new."

14. 1 John 1:6-7, "If we say that we have fellowship with Him, and walk in darkness, we lie and do not practice the truth. But if we walk in the light as He is in the light, we have fellowship with one another, and the blood of Jesus Christ His Son cleanses us from all sin."

15. See Genesis 2:7-19.

16. 1 Chronicles 17:17, "...You [God] have also spoken of Your servant's house [David] for a great while to come, and have regarded me according to the rank of a man of high degree...."

17. Zechariah 9:16, "The Lord their God will save them in that day, as the flock of His people. For they shall be like the jewels of a crown, lifted like a banner over His land."

18. The new birth refers to our spirit. It is a spiritual new birth, a new act of creation carried out by God in humankind, through which sinners receive by grace a new nature, Christ's nature. This implies the forgiveness of our

sins that are erased. When we are born again, we become one spirit with Christ. 1 Corinthians 6:17, "But he who is joined to the Lord is one spirit with Him." This gives us the authority to call God our Father, and to have a Father-son/daughter relationship.

19. Ephesians 2:4-7, "But God, who is rich in mercy, because of His great love with which He loved us, even when we were dead in trespasses, made us alive together with Christ (by grace you have been saved), and raised us up together, and made us sit together in the heavenly places in Christ Jesus, that in the ages to come He might show the exceeding riches of His grace in His kindness toward us in Christ Jesus."

20. Ephesians 6:13-17, "Therefore take up the whole armor of God, that you may be able to withstand in the evil day, and having done all, to stand.... And take the helmet of salvation...." Our minds are the real battlefields, because the enemy tries to convince us not to do what our inner spirits want to do, sowing seeds of doubt. God's armor gives us a helmet to protect us from attacks against our minds. 2 Corinthians 4:4, "...whose minds the god of this age [that is satan] has blinded, who do not believe, lest the light of the gospel of the glory of Christ, who is the image of God, should shine on them." For this reason it is extremely important to study and meditate on the Word. The more truth we know, the more we will be free from being conditioned.

21. See Romans 5:17-19.

22. John 10:10, "The thief does not come except to steal, and to kill, and to destroy. I have come that they may have life, and that they may have it more abundantly."

23. Romans 1:16, "For I [Paul] am not ashamed of the gospel of Christ, for it is the power of God to salvation for everyone who believes, for the Jew first and also for the Greek."

24. To meditate on the Word of God means to let it echo within us, to reflect on what it says, to repeat it softly, to say it to ourselves personalizing it and allowing the Holy Spirit to enlighten us in order to assimilate it. In this way the Gospel influences our whole being: spirit, soul, and body. Psalm 19:14, "Let the words of my mouth and the meditation of my heart be acceptable in Your sight, O Lord, my strength and my Redeemer."

25. Joshua 1:8, "This Book of the Law shall not depart from your mouth, but you shall meditate in it day and night, that you may observe to do according to all that is written in it. For then you will make your way prosperous, and then you will have good success."

26. Romans 13:9-10, "...You shall love your neighbor as yourself. Love does no harm to a neighbor; therefore love is the fulfillment of the law."

27. 2 Timothy 3:16-17, "All Scripture is given by inspiration of God, and is profitable for doctrine, for reproof, for correction, for instruction in righteousness, that the man of God may be complete, thoroughly equipped for every good work."

28. Philippians 4:19, "And my God shall supply all your need according to His riches in glory by Christ Jesus."

29. Acts 3:25-26, "You are sons of the prophets, and of the covenant which God made with our fathers, saying to Abraham, and in your seed all the families of the earth shall be blessed. To you first, God, having raised up His Servant Jesus, sent Him to bless you, in turning away every one of you from your iniquities."

30. Genesis 17:5, "No longer shall your name be called Abram, but your name shall be Abraham; for I have made you a father of many nations."

31. Abram, in Hebrew "Abram" means "elevated, great or exalted father." Abraham, in Hebrew "Abraham," means "father of a great multitude."

32. Exodus 15:26, "and said, 'If you diligently heed the voice of the Lord your God and do what is right in His sight, give ear to His commandments and keep all His statutes, I will put none of the diseases on you which I have brought on the Egyptians. For I am the Lord who heals you.'"

33. Romans 4:16-17, "Therefore *it is of faith*, that it might be by grace; to the end the promise might be sure to all the seed; not to that only which is of the law, but to that also which is of the faith of Abraham; who is the father of us all, (As it is written, I have made thee a father of many nations,) before him whom he believed, even God, who quickeneth the dead, and *calleth those things which be not as though they were*" (KJV).

34. Genesis 39:1, "Now Joseph had been taken down to Egypt. And Potiphar, an officer of Pharaoh, captain of the guard, an Egyptian, bought him from the Ishmaelites who had taken him down there."

35. *To prosper*, from Greek "zalack," which means "to go to the other shore." In other words, *to prosper* means "to succeed in every deed, to arrive at the desired harbor with success, to reach one's aims" (ref. notes taken during lessons held at the Bible School Gesù Vive, at Gesù Vive Church in Baranzate, Milan).

36. See Genesis 37:22-29.

CHAPTER FIVE

1. *Redemption* means deliverance, ransoming, and is the ransom that Jesus paid for each one of us. Colossians 1:13-14, "He has delivered us from the power of darkness and conveyed us into the kingdom of the Son of His love, in whom

we have redemption through His blood, the forgiveness of sins."

2. See Ephesians 6:13-17.

3. Hebrews 8:6, "But now He has obtained a more excellent ministry, inasmuch as He is also Mediator of a better covenant, which was established on better promises." For better comprehension, I suggest reading Hebrews 8, the whole chapter.

4. See 2 Samuel 9:6.

5. Genesis 2:25, "And they were both naked, the man and his wife, and were not ashamed." Genesis 3:7-11, "Then the eyes of both of them were opened, and they knew that they were naked; and they sewed fig leaves together and made themselves coverings. And they heard the sound of the Lord God walking in the garden in the cool of the day, and Adam and his wife hid themselves from the presence of the Lord God among the trees of the garden. Then the Lord God called to Adam and said to him, 'Where are you?' So he said, 'I heard Your voice in the garden, and I was afraid because I was naked; and I hid myself.' And He said, 'Who told you that you were naked?...'"

6. See 2 Samuel 4:4.

7. See 2 Samuel 9:4.

8. Proverbs 3:5-6, "Trust in the Lord with all your heart, and lean not on your own understanding; in all your ways acknowledge Him, and He shall direct your paths."

9. *Justice* from Latin "iustitia," iustus, which means "righteous." The term *justice* is used to indicate that God is righteous and we are righteous in His sight. Deuteronomy 32:4, "He [God] is the Rock, His work is perfect; for all His ways are justice, a God of truth and without injustice; righteous and upright is He." To be righteous means to be in God's presence, in Christ Jesus, without guilt feelings

or sense of condemnation, owing to what Jesus did for us. 1 Corinthians 1:30, "But of Him you are in Christ Jesus, who became for us wisdom from God—and righteousness and sanctification and redemption."

10. Isaiah 45:2-3, "I will go before you and make the crooked places straight; I will break in pieces the gates of bronze and cut the bars of iron. I will give you the treasures of darkness and hidden riches of secret places, that you may know that I, the Lord, who call you by your name, am the God of Israel."

11. See 1 Kings 19:19-21.

12. Ephesians 6:14, "Stand therefore, having girded your waist with truth, having put on the breastplate of righteousness."

13. Ephesians 6:17, "And take the helmet of salvation, and the sword of the Spirit, which is the word of God."

14. Jeremiah 51:11, "Make the arrows bright! Gather the shields! The Lord has raised up the spirit of the kings of the Medes. For His plan is against Babylon to destroy it, because it is the vengeance of the Lord, The vengeance for His temple."

15. See John 10:10.

16. 2 Timothy 4:7, "I have fought the good fight, I have finished the race, I have kept the faith."

17. John 8:31-32, "Then Jesus said to those Jews who believed Him, 'If you abide in My word, you are My disciples indeed. And you shall know the truth, and the truth shall make you free.'"

18. God's Old Testament covenant was a covenant of blood sanctioned by circumcision.

19. See John 20:24-28.

20. 1 John 5:4, "For whatever is born of God overcomes the world. And this is the victory that has overcome the world—our faith."

21. Revelation 3:20, "Behold, I stand at the door and knock. If anyone hears My voice and opens the door, I will come in to him and dine with him, and he with Me."

22. 1 Peter 4:10, "As each one has received a gift, minister it to one another, as good stewards of the manifold grace of God."

23. See Isaiah 53:5; 1 Peter 2:24.

24. Philippians 2:8-10, [Jesus] "being found in appearance as a man, He humbled Himself and became obedient to the point of death, even the death of the cross. Therefore God also has highly exalted Him and given Him the name which is above every name, that at the name of Jesus every knee should bow, of those in heaven, and of those on earth, and of those under the earth."

25. Philippians 4:19, "And my God shall supply all your need according to His riches in glory by Christ Jesus."

26. 2 Timothy 2:13, "If we are faithless, He remains faithful; He cannot deny Himself."

27. Psalm 23:5-6, "You prepare a table before me in the presence of my enemies; You anoint my head with oil; My cup runs over. Surely goodness and mercy shall follow me all the days of my life; and I will dwell in the house of the Lord forever."

28. See Revelation 21:16-23.

29. Mark 11:23-24, "For assuredly, I say to you, whoever says to this mountain, 'Be removed and be cast into the sea,' and does not doubt in his heart, but believes that those things he says will be done, he will have whatever he says. Therefore I

say to you, whatever things you ask when you pray, believe that you receive them, and you will have them."

CHAPTER SIX

1. 1 Samuel 22:5-6, "Now the prophet Gad said to David, 'Do not stay in the stronghold; depart, and go to the land of Judah.' So David departed and went into the forest of Hereth. When Saul heard that David and the men who were with him had been discovered...."

2. Obviously one always extracts the best!

3. See Ezekiel 4:4-13.

4. *To consume* from Latin "consummare," literally means "to accomplish, to fulfill." So the prophets' lives were fulfilled in doing God's will (ref. Dizionario Enciclopedico Italiano Treccani, Italian Encyclopedia).

5. Jeremiah 20:9, "Then I said, 'I will not make mention of Him, nor speak anymore in His name.' But His word was in my heart like a burning fire shut up in my bones; I was weary of holding it back, and I could not."

6. *Compassion* from Latin "compassus," which means "to suffer together." Therefore, God wanted His prophets to have an attitude that showed participation in sufferance (ref. "Il Nuovo Zingarelli," Vocabolario della lingua italiana; Italian Dictionary).

7. 1 Chronicles 4:9-10, "Now Jabez was more honorable than his brothers, and his mother called his name Jabez, saying, 'Because I bore him in pain.' And Jabez called on the God of Israel saying, 'Oh, that You would bless me indeed, and enlarge my territory, that Your hand would be with me, and that You would keep me from evil, that I may not cause pain!' So God granted him what he requested."

8. Romans 8:37-39, "Yet in all these things we are more than conquerors through Him who loved us. For I am persuaded that neither death nor life, nor angels nor principalities nor powers, nor things present nor things to come, nor height nor depth, nor any other created thing, shall be able to separate us from the love of God which is in Christ Jesus our Lord."

9. Before his conversion, his name was Saul.

10. See Acts 7:54-60.

11. Acts 9:3-5, "As he journeyed he came near Damascus, and suddenly a light shone around him from heaven. Then he fell to the ground, and heard a voice saying to him, 'Saul, Saul, why are you persecuting Me?' And he said, 'Who are You, Lord?' Then the Lord said, 'I am Jesus, whom you are persecuting. It is hard for you to kick against the goads.'"

12. That is when we ignored what is right in God's eyes, because we did not know His Word, which is His will for us.

13. In the Bible, to fear God does not mean to be afraid of Him, but rather to respect God, His commandments, and His will.

14. *Accursed*, from Greek "anàthema" which means "curse, to place oneself above." Paul's passion for the work of God and for Jesus was so strong that he was ready to die to see loved ones (relatives and not only) come to the Lord through the blood of Christ.

15. Ecclesiastes 1:18, "For in much wisdom is much grief, and he who increases knowledge increases sorrow."

16. Hebrews 2:18, "For in that He Himself has suffered, being tempted, He is able to aid those who are tempted." 1 Peter 4:1-2, "Therefore, since Christ suffered for us in the flesh, arm yourselves also with the same mind, for he who has suffered in the flesh has ceased from sin, that he no

longer should live the rest of his time in the flesh for the lusts of men, but for the will of God."

17. Ineffable joy is a joy which cannot be expressed in words and goes beyond human experience. It is a divine kind of joy and can be felt only in the Lord's presence.

18. 1 Samuel 22:1, "David therefore departed from there and escaped to the cave of Adullam. So when his brothers and all his father's house heard it, they went down there to him."

19. See 1 Samuel 21:4-7.

20. See 1 Samuel 22:11-18.

21. The ephod was used to consult the Lord to know what to do. From Hebrew "epho(w)dh" which means a "girdle" (Strong's #0641). In the Old Testament Leviticus liturgy, it was the sleeveless priestly robe worn by the high priest. See Exodus 28:6-14.

22. 1 Samuel 22:5, "Now the prophet Gad said to David, 'Do not stay in the stronghold; depart, and go to the land of Judah....'"

23. 1 Corinthians 2:12-15, "Now we have received, not the spirit of the world, but the Spirit who is from God, that we might know the things that have been freely given to us by God. These things we also speak, not in words which man's wisdom teaches but which the Holy Spirit teaches, comparing spiritual things with spiritual. But the natural man does not receive the things of the Spirit of God, for they are foolishness to him; nor can he know them, because they are spiritually discerned. But he who is spiritual judges all things, yet he himself is rightly judged by no one."

24. 1 Samuel 30:3-4, "So David and his men came to the city, and there it was, burned with fire; and their wives, their sons, and their daughters had been taken captive. Then

David and the people who were with him lifted up their voices and wept, until they had no more power to weep."

25. See 1 Samuel 24:9-12.

26. David had the possibility to kill Saul twice, but he did not: "'The Lord forbid that I should do this thing to my master, the Lord's anointed, to stretch out my hand against him, seeing he is the anointed of the Lord.' So David restrained his servants with these words, and did not allow them to rise against Saul. And Saul got up from the cave and went on his way" (1 Samuel 24:6-7).

27. David knew that Saul had been anointed king, therefore he renounced to take the law into his hands and leave space to divine justice: "Therefore let the Lord be judge, and judge between you and me [David], and see and plead my case, and deliver me out of your hand" (1 Samuel 24:15).

28. Since David recognized the divine blessing and the protection on Saul's life, he waited for God's timing. As a consequence, the divine blessing and protection poured out on him.

29. David became an example for others, because when his men saw that despite the opportunities he did not kill Saul, they learned not to carry out revenge themselves. It is God who does justice and puts an end to things. David was a great example in this as well.

CHAPTER SEVEN

1. See 1 Samuel 17:34-37.

2. Psalm 16:8, "I have set the Lord always before me; Because He is at my right hand I shall not be moved."

3. 1 Samuel 22:3, "Then David went from there to Mizpah of Moab...."

4. See Genesis 31:48-53.

5. *Relationship*, from Latin "relazione," *relatus*, past participle of *referre*, which means "to refer." Therefore, to enter into a relationship with God means to refer to Him continuously, to have Him as point of reference (ref. "Nuovo Zingarelli," Vocabolario della lingua italiana; Italian Dictionary).

6. See John 3:1-18.

7. In the Old Testament, by law, only the firstborn inherited the father's wealth as well as the blessing that was on him.

8. See Genesis 25:24-26. Jacob and Esau were twins, but Esau was born first.

9. *Bene - dire*, [to bless] that is to say [dire] – good [bene], to say good things about someone or something.

10. *Male - dire*, [to curse] that is to say [dire] - bad [male], to say bad things about someone or something.

11. Psalm 34:13, "Keep your tongue from evil, and your lips from speaking deceit." Proverbs 6:2, "You are snared by the words of your mouth; you are taken by the words of your mouth."

12. See Genesis 27:1-4.

13. *Jacob* literally means "supplanter, cheater." Esau meant that his brother had the nature of a cheater.

14. The blessing came over Esau anyways, because Isaac said: "You shall live..." and "...when you become restless, that you shall break his yoke from your neck."

15. Mark 9:23, "Jesus said to him, 'If you can believe, all things are possible to him who believes.'"

16. Deuteronomy 28:1-2, "Now it shall come to pass, if you diligently obey the voice of the Lord your God, to observe

carefully all His commandments which I command you today, that the Lord your God will set you high above all nations of the earth. And all these blessings shall come upon you and overtake you...."

17. 1 John 2:21, "...no lie is of the truth." But what is the truth? John 17:17, "Sanctify them by Your truth. Your word is truth." In these verses we clearly read that the Word of God is truth and has no trace of lies in it. The Word contains all of God's promises for our lives.

18. Joshua 1:8, "This Book of the Law shall not depart from your mouth, but you shall meditate in it day and night, that you may observe to do according to all that is written in it. For then you will make your way prosperous, and then you will have good success."

19. Psalm 37:4, "Delight yourself also in the Lord, and He shall give you the desires of your heart."

20. Ephesians 1:3, "Blessed be the God and Father of our Lord Jesus Christ, who has blessed us with every spiritual blessing in the heavenly places in Christ." In order to have a more complete picture of the full blessing that God has destined for each one of us, continue reading Ephesians 1 to verse 14.

21. Hebrews 4:2, "For indeed the gospel was preached to us as well as to them; but the word which they heard did not profit them, not being mixed with faith in those who heard it."

22. Matthew 5:13-15, "You are the salt of the earth; but if the salt loses its flavor, how shall it be seasoned? It is then good for nothing but to be thrown out and trampled underfoot by men. You are the light of the world. A city that is set on a hill cannot be hidden. Nor do they light a lamp and put it under a basket, but on a lampstand, and it gives light to all who are in the house."

23. Psalm 119:105, "Your word is a lamp to my feet and a light to my path."

24. See Ephesians 1:3.

25. Wrong actions are those that stray from the ones described in the Bible as right actions, determined directly by God and taught by Jesus.

26. Romans 5:20-21, "...But where sin abounded, grace abounded much more, so that as sin reigned in death, even so grace might reign through righteousness to eternal life through Jesus Christ our Lord." Romans 6:1-2, "What shall we say then? Shall we continue in sin that grace may abound? Certainly not!..."

27. *Restore*—this verb comes from the Latin verb *restaurare*, which means "to restore/return art works or other manufactures to their primitive state, remaking them, repairing them or renovating them." So when God says that He shall restore you, He is saying that He will bring you back to the original state, that is to His own image, because we were created in His image and likeness (ref. "Il Nuovo Zingarelli," Vocabolario della lingua italiana; Italian Dictionary).

28. Deuteronomy 28:12, "The Lord will open to you His good treasure, the heavens, to give the rain to your land in its season, and to bless all the work of your hand...." Jesus is God made man. In the person of Jesus, God spontaneously decided to divest Himself for us of His riches— eternity, omniscience, omnipresence, almightiness and all of His glory. These are eternal riches!

29. Luke 8:1-3, "Now it came to pass, afterward, that He went through every city and village, preaching and bringing the glad tidings of the kingdom of God. And the twelve were with Him, and certain women who had been healed of evil spirits and infirmities—Mary called Magdalene, out of whom had come seven demons, and Joanna

the wife of Chuza, Herod's steward, and Susanna, and many others who provided for Him from their substance."

30. Isaiah 53:5, "But He was wounded for our transgressions, He was bruised for our iniquities; the chastisement for our peace was upon Him, and by His stripes we are healed." Mentioned also in 1 Peter 2:24.

31. Mark 11:22-24, "So Jesus answered and said to them, Have faith in God. For assuredly, I say to you, whoever says to this mountain, 'Be removed and be cast into the sea,' and does not doubt in his heart, but believes that those things he says will be done, he will have whatever he says. Therefore I say to you, whatever things you ask when you pray, believe that you receive them, and you will have them."

CHAPTER EIGHT

1. Luke 21:33, "Heaven and earth will pass away, but My words will by no means pass away." Romans 4:20-21, "He [Abraham] did not waver at the promise of God through unbelief, but was strengthened in faith, giving glory to God, and being fully convinced that what He had promised He was also able to perform." Hebrews 10:23, "Let us hold fast the confession of our hope without wavering, for He who promised is faithful."

2. Romans 10:17, "So then faith comes by hearing, and hearing by the word of God."

3. John 3:16-17, "For God so loved the world that He gave His only begotten Son, that whoever believes in Him should not perish but have everlasting life. For God did not send His Son into the world to condemn the world, but that the world through Him might be saved."

4. Revelation 1:5-6, "...Jesus Christ, the faithful witness, the firstborn from the dead, and the ruler over the kings of

the earth. …and has made us kings and priests to His God and Father…"

5. Ignorance always in the sense of *ignoring* what is written in the Word.

6. See Genesis 19:1-24.

7. See Acts 5:17-23; 12:7-11.

8. Ephesians 6:16, "…above all, taking the shield of faith with which you will be able to quench all the fiery darts of the wicked one." To learn about the whole armor that God has given us, read Ephesians 6:13-18.

9. 1 John 5:4, "For whatever is born of God overcomes the world. And this is the victory that has overcome the world—our faith."

10. Romans 1:16, "For I am not ashamed of the gospel of Christ, for it is the power of God to salvation for everyone who believes, for the Jew first and also for the Greek."

11. Centro di Formazione Biblica Rhema-Italia; website www.rhemaitalia.it.

12. Matthew 10:30, "But the very hairs of your head are all numbered."

13. Luke 15:10, "Likewise, I say to you, there is joy in the presence of the angels of God over one sinner who repents."

14. Psalm 16:11, "You will show me the path of life; in Your presence is fullness of joy; at Your right hand are pleasures forevermore."

15. See Hebrews 1:3-14.

16. See 1 Corinthians 12:7-11.

17. 1 Corinthians 6:19-20, "Or do you not know that your body is the temple of the Holy Spirit who is in you, whom

you have from God, and you are not your own? For you were bought at a price; therefore glorify God in your body and in your spirit, which are God's."

18. Romans 10:10, "For with the heart one believes unto righteousness, and with the mouth confession is made unto salvation."

ABOUT THE AUTHOR

Pastor Angelo Scannapieco is a man with broad vision and great faithfulness and passion in proclaiming and teaching the Gospel. He grew up serving his local church with loyalty, and was conferred his Bible school Diploma under Tony Cameneti's and Patsy Behrman's guidance.

In 1994, following his calling as pastor, he started the Evangelical Christian Church Gesù Vive in Milan, Italy, now located in a new building in Baranzate.

As of 1999, he has been teaching at Rhema Bible Training Center-Italy, from which he has received an honorary appreciation.

In addition to *Choose Your Destiny*, he has also written *Gli affinché di Dio* [The "So That" of God]. He teaches in several Bible schools in Italy, and is a very much appreciated speaker with a high sensitivity toward the Holy Spirit's guidance.

Spurred by the vision to announce the Word and the new birth in homes and in people's lives, he has started many initiatives throughout the years, including: weekly teaching and edification meetings in family cells; a three-year Bible school addressed to his church members; promoter and person in charge of the annual European Faith Conference (Convegno Europeo della Fede); founder of the Ibi-Rhema Itinerating Bible School (Istituto Biblico Itinerante Ibi-Rhema), and host of the weekly television program "Beyond the Mountains" (Oltre le montagne) on Christian television TBNE.

Pastor Scannapieco is very much involved in missionary and study trips around the world obeying to what the Word says:

> *Sanctify them by Your truth. Your word is truth. As You sent Me into the world, I also have sent them into the world. And for their sakes I sanctify Myself, that they also may be sanctified by the truth. I do not pray for these alone, but also for those who will believe in Me through their word; that they all may be one, as You, Father, are in Me, and I in You; that they also may be one in Us, that the world may believe that You sent Me. And the glory which You gave Me I have given them, that they may be one just as We are one: I in them, and You in Me; that they may be made perfect in one, and that the world may know that You have sent Me, and have loved them as You have loved Me (John 17:17-23).*

In the ministry, he collaborates with his wife, Pastor Chiara, who is a strong and excellent support in pastoring the local church, and with whom he shares the same passion and vision for spreading the Word throughout the world. Pastor Chiara is the worship leader at Gesù Vive and has been teaching at Rhema Bible Training Center-Italy since 2000, from which she has received an honorary appreciation as well. She teaches at the prayer school she founded in the local church, and is often called to speak in conferences organized throughout the country. Her love in proclaiming the Word drove her to write and create the musical "Ruth, the Pearl of Moab," which has obtained great reviews and audience success.

Another exciting book from
Evangelista Media™

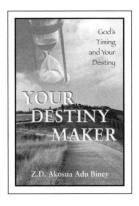

YOUR DESTINY MAKER
God's Timing and Your Destiny

by *Z.D. Akosua Adu Biney*

God is ready, willing, and able to help you fulfill your destiny in cooperation and obedience with Him in this time, regardless of your human abilities and qualifications.

The exceptional nuggets of wisdom within this book will give you a startling sense of God speaking directly to you.

The vibrant energy and veritable gems of truth will stop you where you are, spur you to reassess your life, and stimulate you to strive toward the higher calling that God has for you.

This prayerfully and carefully picked assortment of themes will capture your heart and captivate your spirit.

ISBN: 978-88-96727-68-3

Order now from Evangelista Media™
Telephone: +39 085 4716623 • Fax +39 085 9090113
Email: orders@evangelistamedia.com
Internet: www.evangelistamedia.com

Another exciting book from
EVANGELISTA MEDIA™

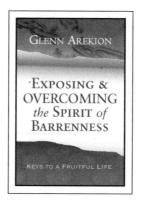

EXPOSING & OVERCOMING THE SPIRIT OF BARRENNESS
Keys to a Fruitful Life

by *Glenn Arekion*

Many Christians are unaware of the spirit of barrenness in their lives. It can stealthily slither into every aspect of life including your health, finances, emotions, family, and career. But there is good news! If you can expose this deadly spirit, you can break the chains keeping you from living the life God intended for you to enjoy.

No longer will you be controlled by the spirit of barrenness—you can lead a life of abundance and fruitfulness, beginning today!

ISBN: 978-88-96727-92-8

Another exciting book from
EVANGELISTA MEDIA™

BUILD REAL WEALTH
Practical Steps to Regain Financial Stability
by *Sam Adeyemi*

In good times and in bad times, you can Build Real Wealth!

Build Real Wealth brings a fresh perspective to the subject of financial prosperity. Real money is not paper—it is value, something you cannot see with your eyes. There is a much deeper dimension to money than the hundred-dollar bill.

Pastor and author Sam Adeyemi has successfully applied the insights in *Build Real Wealth* with outstanding results in his life and ministry. He has taught them to hundreds of audiences with exciting transformations in the finances of thousands of people.

Now it is your turn for God to take you into higher dimensions in your finances as the blessing of Abraham becomes your tangible reality.

ISBN: 978-88-96727-64-5

Order now from Evangelista Media™
Telephone: +39 085 4716623 • Fax +39 085 9090113
Email: orders@evangelistamedia.com
Internet: www.evangelistamedia.com

Additional copies of this book and other book
titles from EVANGELISTA MEDIA™
and DESTINY IMAGE™ EUROPE
are available at your local bookstore.

We are adding new titles every month!

To view our complete catalog online, visit us at:
www.evangelistamedia.com

Send a request for a catalog to:

Via della Scafa, 29/14
65013 Città Sant'Angelo (Pe), ITALY
Tel. +39 085 4716623 • Fax +39 085 9090113
info@evangelistamedia.com

"Changing the World, One Book at a Time."

Are you an author?
Do you have a "today" God-given message?

CONTACT US

We will be happy to review your manuscript
for the possibility of publication:

publisher@evangelistamedia.com
http://www.evangelistamedia.com/pages/AuthorsAppForm.htm